plain ~~~~ ~~~
gobel but not ~
not effective, n~
but not evil ~~
intention,
intention a~
acquiant
a intention to be how which
is her form of consciously
tasting flavors. Absolutely
no distinguishing sense
for people. Self knowledge

TWO LIVES

TWO LIVES

GERTRUDE AND ALICE

JANET MALCOLM

Yale University Press   New Haven & London

Designed by James J. Johnson and set in Monotype
Scotch Roman type by Integrated Publishing Solutions.
Printed in the United States of America.

Library of Congress Cataloging-in-Publication Data

Malcolm, Janet.
    Two lives : Gertrude and Alice / Janet Malcolm.
        p.   cm.
    Includes bibliographical references.
    ISBN 978-0-300-12551-1 (alk. paper)

    1. Stein, Gertrude, 1874–1946.   2. Toklas, Alice B.
3. Authors, American—20th century—Biography.
4. Americans—France—Paris—History—20th century.
5. Paris (France)—Intellectual life—20th century.
I. Title.
    PS3537.T323Z7137 2007
    818'.5209—dc22
    [B]

                                                    2007012085

A catalogue record for this book is available from the
British Library.

The paper in this book meets the guidelines for permanence and
durability of the Committee on Production Guidelines for Book
Longevity of the Council on Library Resources.

10   9   8   7   6   5   4   3   2   1

Frontispiece: Gertrude Stein and Alice B. Toklas on the terrace
at Bilignin, 1936. Photograph by Cecil Beaton.

Portions of this work were originally published in
the *New Yorker*.

To Ann Arensberg

The endearing elegance of female friendship

—SAMUEL JOHNSON

Rasselas, chapter 46

CONTENTS

PART ONE

When I read *The Alice B. Toklas Cook Book* for the first time, Eisenhower was in the White House and Liz Taylor had taken Eddie Fisher away from Debbie Reynolds. The book, published in 1954, was given to me by a fellow member of a group of pretentious young persons I ran around with, who had nothing but amused contempt for middlebrow American culture, and whose revolt against the conformity of the time largely took the form of patronizing a furniture store called Design Research and of writing mannered letters to each other modeled on the mannered letters of certain famous literary homosexuals, not then known as such. *The*

Alice B. Toklas Cook Book fit right in with our program of callow preciousness; we loved its waspishly magisterial tone, its hauteur and malice. "The French never add Tabasco, ketchup or Worcestershire sauce, nor do they eat any of the innumerable kinds of pickles, nor do they accompany a meat course with radishes, olives or salted nuts," Toklas wrote, as if preparing a manifesto for us. Her *de haut en bas* footnote pointing out that "a marinade is a bath of wine, herbs, oil, vegetables, vinegars and so on, in which fish or meat destined for particular dishes repose for specified periods and acquire virtue" filled us with ecstasy.

The *Cook Book* itself sits in a kind of bath of reminiscence about Toklas's life with Gertrude Stein, from which its own literary virtue derives. More than a cookbook and memoir, it could almost be called a work of literary modernism, a sort of pendant to Stein's tour de force *The Autobiography of Alice B. Toklas,* published in 1933. The similarity of tone of the two books only deepens the mystery of who influenced whom. Was Stein imitating Toklas when she wrote in Toklas's voice in the *Autobiography,* or did she invent the voice, and did Toklas then imitate Stein's invention when she wrote the *Cook Book?* It is impossible to say.

Leafing through my copy of the *Cook Book,* the evidence of ancient food stains leads me to the recipes I actually cooked, and there are not many of them. Most of Toklas's recipes were and remain too elaborate or too strange to attempt (I did make—loving its perversity— her Gigot de la Clinique, which involved taking a large hypodermic needle and injecting a leg of lamb twice daily for a week with orange juice as it sat in the obligatory marinade of wine and herbs). Underlinings and marginal comments also highlight the passages—such as those quoted above—whose tart snottiness gave me special delight in the fifties. But there is one chapter whose pages bear no gravy stains or underlinings and whose bare cleanness makes it look almost unread. It is entitled "Food in the Bugey during the Occupation," and in it Toklas writes of the years of the Nazi occupation, which she and Stein spent in an area of provincial eastern France called the

Bugey—first in a handsome old house near the town of Belley, and then in another old house in nearby Culoz. When I had occasion to read this chapter again, I was struck by its evasiveness, no less than by its painfully forced gaiety. How had the pair of elderly Jewish lesbians escaped the Nazis? Why had they stayed in France instead of returning to the safety of the United States? Why did Toklas omit any mention of her and Stein's Jewishness (never mind lesbianism)? Well, in the fifties one did not go out of one's way to mention one's Jewishness. Gentlemanly anti-Semitism was still a fact of American life. The fate of Europe's Jews was known, but the magnitude of the catastrophe had not registered; the term "Holocaust" was not yet in use. In 1954, Toklas's evasions went as unremarked as her recipes for A Restricted Veal Loaf and Swimming Crawfish went uncooked. Today, the evasions seem egregious, though hardly incomprehensible. What we now know about Stein's and Toklas's war makes it easy to see why the complex actuality of their situation and conduct found no place

in *The Alice B. Toklas Cook Book.* "As if a cookbook has anything to do with writing," Toklas
says of her enterprise at the book's end. Or
with complexity, she might have added.

In August 1924, while driving to the French
Riviera to visit Picasso, Stein and Toklas
veered over to the Bugey and spent a night in
Belley at a hotel called the Pernollet, which
had been recommended to them for its good
food. The food turned out to be mediocre, but
they liked the hotel and the countryside so well
that they stayed on—wiring Picasso that they
would be delayed a week, and finally never
making it to the Riviera at all. Stein and Toklas returned to the Pernollet summer after
summer (eating elsewhere) and presently began
looking for a place of their own in the region.
They were prepared to buy, build, or rent, but
could find nothing that suited. Then one day,
across a valley, they saw "the house of our
dreams," as Gertrude Stein writes in the *Autobiography*, and continues:

Go and ask the farmer there whose house that is, Gertrude Stein said to me. I said, nonsense it is an important house and it is occupied. Go and ask him, she said. Very reluctantly I did. He said, well yes, perhaps it is for rent, it belongs to a little girl, all her people are dead and I think there is a lieutenant of the regiment stationed in Belley living there now, but I understand they were to leave. You might go and see the agent of the property. We did, He was a kindly old farmer who always told us allez doucement, go slowly. We did. We had the promise of the house, which we never saw any nearer than across the valley, as soon as the lieutenant should leave. Finally three years ago the lieutenant went to Morocco and we took the house still only having seen it from across the valley and we have liked it always more.

Stein wrote *The Autobiography of Alice B. Toklas* in the fall of 1932 in a kind of paroxysm of desire for the fame and money that had so far eluded her. Since her youth, she had wanted "gloire," as her friend Mabel Weeks reported, but her experimental writings had not brought it. Finally, at the age of fifty-eight, she decided to (so to speak) prostitute herself and write a book in regular English that would be a best seller. That it actually became one may be a measure of the genius Stein claims for herself throughout the book. What kind of a genius she was is hard to pin down. She had trained to become a medical doctor, specializing in psychology, and only after dropping out of the Johns Hopkins medical school in her last year, in 1901, did she begin to think of writing as her conduit to glory. Her apprentice work was conventional and unpromising, rather stilted. After she settled in Paris, in 1903, however, as if her muse were finally roused by the Old World's more bracing air, she began to produce the writings for which she is known—stories, novels, and poems that are like no stories, novels, or poems ever written but seem to be saturated with some sort of elixir of originality. In the trio of stories *Three Lives,* written in 1905, and the novel *The Making of Americans,* begun in 1903 and completed in 1911, Stein is still writing in regular, if singular English, but by 1912 she had started producing work in a language of her own, one that uses English words but in no other way resembles English as it is known. "Not to be wrapped and then to forget undertaking, the credit and then the resting of that interval, the pressing of the sounding when there is no trinket is not altering, there can be pleasing classing clothing," she writes in "Portrait of Mabel Dodge at Villa Curonia" (1912), an early foray into this language. (The ostensible subject of the portrait—a rich American adventuress who had entertained Stein and Toklas at her Italian villa—was so taken with the piece that she had it privately printed and bound in Florentine wallpaper, and handed it out to visitors at her Fifth Avenue apartment.) Two years later, in "Tender Buttons," inspired by Cubist still-lifes, Stein raises the stakes:

A BOX

Out of kindness comes redness and out of rudeness comes rapid same question, out of an eye comes research, out of selection comes painful cattle. So then the order is that a white way of being round is something suggesting a

pin and is it disappointing, it is not, it is so
rudimentary to be analyzed and see a fine sub-
stance strangely, it is so earnest to have a
green point not to red but to point again.

APPLE

Apple plum, carpet steak, seed clam, colored
wine, calm seen, cold cream, best shake, potato, potato and no no gold work with pet, a
green seen is called bake and change sweet is
bready, a little piece a little piece please.

A little piece please. Cane again to the pre-
supposed and ready eucalyptus tree, count
out sherry and ripe plates and little corners of
a kind of ham. This is use.

ORANGE

Why is a feel oyster an egg stir. Why is it
orange centre.

A show at tick and loosen loosen it so to
speak sat.

It was an extra leaker with a see spoon, it
was an extra licker with a see spoon.

In a piece entitled "An Acquaintance with Description," written in 1926, the wordplay achieves a graphic dimension:

> Let it be when it is mine to be sure let it be when it is mine when it is mine let it be to be sure when it is mine to be sure let it be let it be let it be to be sure let it be to be sure when it is mine to be sure let it to be sure when it is mine let it be to be sure let it be to be sure to be sure let it be to be sure let it be to be sure to be sure let it be to be sure let it be to be sure let it be to be sure let it be mine to be sure let it be to be sure to be mine to be sure to be mine to be sure to be mine let it be to be mine let it be to be sure to be mine to be sure let it be to be mine let it be to be sure let it be to be sure to be sure let it be sure mine to be sure let it be mine to let it be to be sure to let it be it to be sure mine to be sure let it be mine to let it be to be sure to let it be mine when to be sure when to be sure to let it to be sure to be mine.

The unflagging inventiveness of Stein's language experiments, and the consistent authority of her tone, brought her ever greater renown in the world of the avant-garde. But this wasn't enough for her—she wanted to conquer the large outer world as well.

With *The Autobiography of Alice B. Toklas* she not only achieved the vulgar celebrity she craved but brilliantly solved the koan of autobiography by disclaiming responsibility for the one being written. Speaking in the voice of her companion, Gertrude Stein can entirely dispense with the fiction of humility that the conventional autobiographer must at every moment struggle to maintain. "I must say that only three times in my life have I met a genius," Stein has Toklas say of their first meeting, "and each time a bell within me rang and I was not mistaken, and I may say in each case it was before there was any general recognition of the quality of genius in them. The three geniuses of whom I wish to speak are Gertrude Stein, Pablo Picasso and Alfred Whitehead."

Stein's playful egomania pervades the book ("she realizes that in English literature in her time she is the only one"), as does an optimism that gives the story of her life the character of a fairy tale. Nothing bad ever happens to her;

every difficulty is overcome as if by magic.
While a student at Radcliffe in the late 1890s,
faced with an examination in William James's
philosophy course for which she has not stud-
ied, Stein writes on the examination paper:
"Dear Professor James, I am so sorry but really I do not feel a bit like an examination
paper in philosophy today," and leaves the examination room. The next day she receives
a postcard from James: "Dear Miss Stein, I
understand perfectly how you feel. I often feel
like that myself"—and he gives her the high-
est grade in the course. Her whole life is like
that. Picasso is going to paint her portrait but
after eighty or ninety sittings, he says, "I can't
see you any longer when I look," irritably
paints out the face, and goes to Spain for a va-
cation. On his return, he paints in the face
from memory and presents Stein with the famous masklike portrait. Or here is how Stein
and Toklas came to work as volunteers during World War I, driving supplies to regional
French hospitals (work for which they were
decorated by the French government): "One
day we were walking down the rue des Pyra-

Gertrude Stein with Picasso's portrait, 1922.
Photograph by Man Ray.

mides and there was a ford car being backed up
the street by an american girl and on the car it
said, American Fund for French Wounded. . . .
We went over and talked to the american girl
and then interviewed Mrs. Lathrop, the head
of the organization. She was enthusiastic, she
was always enthusiastic and she said, get a car.
But where, we asked. From America, she said.
But how, we said. Ask somebody, she said, and
Gertrude Stein did, she asked her cousin and in
a few months the ford car came."

The story of the acquisition of "the house
of our dreams" is the culminating example
of life's evident inability ever to say no to
Gertrude Stein. But the story doesn't end
there. Four years after the publication of *The
Autobiography of Alice B. Toklas* Stein wrote
another autobiography, called *Everybody's Autobiography.* The intention was both to repeat
the success of the best seller and to atone for it.
Naturally, only the second intention was fulfilled. What Stein felt she had to atone for
was the crisp linear narrative of *The Autobiography of Alice B. Toklas,* which she had adopted
merely in order to woo the conventional read-

ing public, and which was not her style at all.
Now, writing in her own voice, Stein no longer
feels constrained to attend to the reader's
wants. She reverts to her old way of writing as
if the reader were an uninvited guest arriving
on the wrong night at a dark house. The idea
this time is not to shape life into a narrative of
gay and triumphant wish fulfillment but to
present it in all its elusive ambiguity. In *Everybody's Autobiography* Stein again tells the story
of the acquisition of the dream house, but now
it is a confession of bad behavior. The house
did not just fall into the hands of Stein and
Toklas. They went to ruthless lengths to wrest
it from the lieutenant—lengths that seem more
connected to savage twenty-first-century New
York real estate practice than to civilized
twentieth-century literary history. Stein begins the story with characteristic indirectness:

> The present tenant was a lieutenant in the
> army and as he was stationed at the garrison
> in Belley, they have a battalion of Moroccan
> troops there, it is always strange to see in a
> mountain French village these native troops.

It is queer the use of the word, native always means people who belong somewhere else, because they had once belonged somewhere else. That shows that the white race does not really think they belong anywhere because they think of everybody else as a native. Anyway the lieutenant who was in the house that we had seen across the valley and that we had had to have was stationed in the garrison at Belley. . . . Why said everybody do you not get him made captain, then he would have to leave as there is no room for another captain there in the garrison. We thought that an excellent idea. . . .

Well we know a man he is a nice man his name is George. . . . When he was doing his military service he was clerk in the war office. He used to tell how every one even a general would come in and ask him if he could not get something done a little quicker for him. . . .

George went off and after some months of waiting in which you look anxious but ask no questions and he mysteriously said wait he came and said I have bad news for you, they say at the war office that he is not much good as a lieutenant, he is a war lieutenant, and cannot pass any further examinations but as a

captain he would not do at all and then be-
sides when he retired he would have to be paid
a pension as a captain and now in two or three
years he retires and they only have to pay his
pension as a lieutenant, but said George perhaps he could go to Morocco that would be
good for him he would get more money for
active service and he would leave the house
free. . . . A month after the proprietor wrote
and said the lieutenant was going to Morocco
and was ready to sublet the house to us.

In *The Alice B. Toklas Cook Book,* Toklas
retells the story, changing some of the details,
and promoting the lieutenant to captain, but
essentially corroborating Stein's version. What
actually happened remains unclear. Stein and
Toklas's unrepentant confession of pushing the
lieutenant (or captain) out of the house has
the ring of truth, but is full of holes. It raises
more questions than it answers. The expatri-
ate writer and editor Elliot Paul, in his book
Understanding the French (1954), offers an illuminating, if rather extreme, example of what
happens to historical accounts that don't add
up: they get rewritten so that they do. Paul au-

daciously takes Stein and Toklas's meshugener
story and changes it into a plausible narrative:

> It was four miles from Belley where Gertrude
> Stein had her country residence, a house she
> wanted so badly before she could buy it that
> she went to the Secretary of War himself, in
> order to pave the way for the deal. The house
> was occupied by a major [yet another promo-
> tion] who had been overlooked two or three
> times, for one reason or another, when promo-
> tions were in order. The major would not sell
> his house for any price unless he was made a
> lieutenant-colonel and transferred to North
> Africa. Now Gertrude, with Alice Toklas, had
> performed such heroic ambulance-driving duty
> in World I that she had been cited and deco-
> rated by the same Secretary of War, who was
> still in office when she coveted the Major's little
> house. Gertrude, always a woman of direct ac-
> tion in the higher echelons, went straight to the
> Secretary and asked him to arrange the Major's
> promotion, which he did.

Stein, of course, never went to the Secretary of War, nor did she buy the house—it was
not for sale but for lease. Paul's assertion about

the major's refusal to sell unless he was promoted and sent to Africa is fantasy. But Paul
was right to stress how badly the women wanted
the place. The house (by no means little) was a
seventeenth-century stone manor, situated in
the hamlet of Bilignin, a few miles from Belley.
It had outbuildings, vegetable gardens, fruit
trees, and a terrace garden that looked out
over the valley toward the distant mountains.
Inside were spacious rooms with old wall-
papers and antique furniture. The couple came
there every spring and stayed until the fall—
later and later into the fall as time went on.
The place was "better than our dreams of it,"
Toklas wrote in the *Cook Book*. Friends would
visit and take photographs, and these, even in
black and white, capture the extraordinary
beauty of the place and testify to the content-
ment of its inhabitants.

When war came to Europe in the fall of
1939 the couple were at Bilignin and remained
there for the winter. Stein "wheedled a military pass from the authorities," Toklas writes
in the *Cook Book*, so that they could drive to
Paris to get winter clothes and passports from

Gertrude Stein and Alice B. Toklas with Picasso on the
terrace at Bilignin, early 1930s.

their apartment, and to try to protect Stein's great modernist paintings against bombing by laying them out on the floor. That attempt was abandoned—"the wall space was four times larger than floor space"—nor could they find the passports, which had been put away too well. Writing of their search, Toklas lets drop a chilling detail. In the hunt for the passports, the pedigree of their poodle Basket turned up. "I put it in my bag," she writes. "Later the authorities gave a ration to pedigreed dogs and Basket was not too badly nourished during the years of restriction." So the Nazi racial theories extended even to pets.

Between 1939 and 1940 Stein and Toklas constantly wavered on the question of whether to stay in France or go back to America. In an article published in the *Atlantic Monthly* in 1940, called "The Winner Loses: A Picture of Occupied France," Stein records the tenseness of the time. When Italy came into the war in June 1940, "I was scared, completely scared, and my stomach felt very weak, because—well, here we were right in everybody's path. . . . I was frightened; I woke up completely upset.

And I said to Alice Toklas, 'Let's go away.' . . . And we telephoned to the American consul in Lyon and he said, 'I'll fix up your passports. Do not hesitate—leave.'" But the next day, on the way back from seeing the consul in Lyon, who again told them to leave in no uncertain terms, "I said to Alice Toklas, 'Well, I don't know—it would be awfully uncomfortable and I am fussy about my food. Let's not leave.'" After further vacillations and another trip to Lyon, the decision to stay was made. It came about this way: returning from Lyon, as they approached Belley, Stein and Toklas met a local doctor named Chaboux and his wife, and put their dilemma to him.

> "Well," said Doctor Chaboux, reflecting, "I can't guarantee you anything, but my advice is stay. I had friends," he said, "who in the last war stayed in their homes all through the German occupation, and they saved their homes and those who left lost theirs. No," he said, "I think unless your house is actually destroyed by a bombardment, I always think the best thing to do is to stay." He went on, "Everybody knows you here; everybody likes you; we

all would help you in every way. Why risk
yourself among strangers?"

"Thank you," we said, "that is all we need.
We stay."

In her book *Wars I Have Seen* (written between the winter of 1942–43 and the summer
of 1944, and published in 1945), Stein records
another scary moment of decision, one that
took place in February 1943. She and Toklas
were about to move house from Bilignin to a
manor in Culoz a few miles away, and had gone
to Belley to say good-bye to a lawyer who had
represented them in an unsuccessful lawsuit
against the owner of the Bilignin house, who
had reclaimed it for her own use. (When
friends found them the house in Culoz, they
abandoned a second lawsuit.) "My lawyer said
that everything was nicely arranged and we
thanked each other and said what a pleasure it
had all been," Stein writes, and then gets to
her point:

and now I have something rather serious to
tell you [the lawyer said]. I was in Vichy yes-

terday, and I saw Maurice Sivain. Sivain had
been sous-prefet at Belley and had been most
kind and helpful in extending our privileges
and our occupation of our house, and Maurice
Sivain said to me, tell these ladies that they
must leave at once for Switzerland, tomorrow
if possible otherwise they will be put into a
concentration camp. But I said we are just
moving. I know he said. I felt very funny,
quite completely funny. But how can we go, as
the frontier is closed, I said. That he said
could be arranged, I think that could be
arranged. You mean pass by fraud I said, Yes
he said, it could be arranged. I felt very funny.

Stein goes home and says to Toklas,

We are not moving tomorrow we are going to
Switzerland . . . and Alice Toklas and I sat
down to supper. We both felt funny and then I
said. No, I am not going we are not going, it is
better to go regularly wherever we are sent
than to go irregularly where nobody can help
us if we are in trouble, no I said, they are always trying to get us to leave France but here
we are and here we stay. What do you think, I
said, and we thought and I said we will walk

down to Belley and see the lawyer and tell him no . . . the lawyer said perhaps we had better go and then he said he had a house way up in the mountains and there nobody would know, and I said well perhaps later but now I said to-morrow we are going to move to Culoz, with our large comfortable new house with two good servants and a nice big park with trees, and we all went home, and we did move the next day. It took us some weeks to get over it but we finally did.

Stein's refusal to budge in the face of such a warning is at once incredible and completely in character. Early in *Wars I Have Seen*—in fact on its first page—Stein presents herself to the reader in such a way as to make her behavior comprehensible and consistent with the deep structures of her personality. She tells us that she was the youngest of five children, the baby of the family, "and as such naturally I had privileges the privilege of petting the privilege of being the youngest one. If that does happen it is not lost all the rest of one's life, there you are you are privileged, nobody can do anything but take care of you, that is the way I was and this is the way I still am, and any one who is like that necessarily liked it. I did and do."

Nobody can do anything but take care of you. Throughout her life, Stein was taken care of by people who evidently felt helpless to do otherwise. The chief of these worker bees was Alice Toklas, who managed the practical details of Stein's life almost to the point of parody. In *Everybody's Autobiography*—a large part of which is taken up with Stein's lecture tour in America after the triumph of *The Autobiography of Alice B. Toklas*—Stein herself pokes fun at her dependence on Toklas:

> I liked the photographers, there is one who came in and said he was sent to do a layout of me. A layout, I said yes he said what is that I said oh he said it is four or five pictures of you doing anything. All right I said what do you want me to do. Why he said there is your airplane bag suppose you unpack it oh I said Miss Toklas always does that oh no I could not do that, well he said there is the telephone suppose you telephone well I said yes but I never do Miss Toklas always does that, well he said what can you do, well I said I can put my

> hat on and take my hat off and I can put my
> coat on and I can take it off and I like water I
> can drink a glass of water all right he said do
> that so I did that and he photographed while
> I did that.

In the *Cook Book*, Toklas takes the joke a
step further when she exclaims of an incon-
venient gift of pigeons, "Six white pigeons to
be smothered, to be plucked, to be cleaned and
all this to be accomplished before Gertrude
Stein returned, for she didn't like to see work
being done." But the work Toklas did for Stein
was no joke. It was unending and evidently
ungrudging.

"I had cajoling ways, one has when one
continues to be the youngest," Stein writes of
herself as a child in *Wars I Have Seen,* and these
ways never left her. Her charm was as conspic-
uous as her fatness, and surely accounts for
the way people were always practically lining
up to be of service to her—not only Alice Toklas and friends such as Carl Van Vechten and
Mabel Dodge and Thornton Wilder but perfect
strangers. Writing in the *Autobiography* of the

period in World War I when she was driving the
Ford car from the obliging cousin, Stein has
Toklas report that "she never did anything for
herself, neither changing a tyre, cranking the
car or repairing it," because someone else always turned up. Stein/Toklas continues:

> This faculty of Gertrude Stein of having every-
> body do anything for her puzzled the other
> drivers of the organization. Mrs. Lathrop who
> used to drive her own car said that nobody did
> these things for her. It was not only soldiers, a
> chauffeur would get off the seat of a private
> car in the place Vendome and crank Stein's old
> ford for her. Gertrude Stein said that the oth-
> ers looked so efficient, of course nobody would
> think of doing anything for them. Now as for
> herself she was not efficient, she was good hu-
> mored, she was democratic, one person was
> as good as another, and she knew what she
> wanted done. If you are like that she says,
> anybody will do anything for you. The impor-
> tant thing, she insists, is that you must have
> deep down as the deepest thing in you a sense
> of equality. Then anybody will do anything
> for you.

This is pretty irresistible. But one should not make the mistake of assigning to Stein's rhetoric of equality and one person being as good as another its usual left-wing label. Stein was a conservative with an increasingly reactionary bent—she loved the Republican Party, she hated Roosevelt, and she actually supported Franco. "She was a rentier, and possessed a rentier mentality in matters of taxes, jobs, and governments," a young American friend, W. G. Rogers, wrote of Stein in a memoir entitled *When This You See Remember Me: Gertrude Stein in Person* (1948). He went on: "Without her fixed income we might never have heard of the rue de Fleurus, but with it we should not be surprised to find her disapproving of Roosevelt and the New Deal, believing in rugged individualism, favoring a gold basis for the dollar, regarding a man out of work as lazy or incompetent, thinking every American always could take care of himself."

The equality Stein was talking about was her youngest-child's confidence that everyone was susceptible to her charm. She could chat up anyone. But she surely did not believe that

one person was as good as another. The issue of
superiority—of who was a genius, as she put it,
and who wasn't—was of abiding interest to
her. Stein's snobbery began in childhood. She
was contemptuous of two of her four siblings—
her brother Simon (second-born) and her sister
Bertha (third-born)—viewing the former as
simpleminded and pathetic and the latter as
boring and annoying. ("It is natural not to care
about a sister certainly not when she is four
years older and grinds her teeth at night.") She
respected the oldest brother, Michael, who
took over the family business when the father,
Daniel Stein, died in 1891 (he was part owner
of several San Francisco street railroads),
and who made the fixed income possible; and
she adored the fourth-born, Leo, who was
two years her senior and brilliantly intelligent.
"My brother and I were always together,"
Stein recalls in *Everybody's Autobiography,* and
goes on to observe: "It is better if you are the
youngest girl in a family to have a brother two
years older because that makes everything
a pleasure to you, you go everywhere and do
everything while he does it all for and with you

Gertrude and Leo Stein at Harvard, ca. 1897.

which is a pleasant way to have everything
happen to you." When Leo went to Harvard,
Gertrude followed him to Radcliffe; while she
was at medical school at Johns Hopkins, he
took up a scientific research project in Baltimore; and when he moved to Paris in 1903, she
joined him in his quarters at 27 rue de Fleurus,
where she began to pursue her writing career in
earnest and, under Leo's tutelage, to see the
point of modernist art and to become a fellow
early collector of it. But then Leo, too, was
found wanting. "Slowly and in a way it was not
astonishing but slowly I was knowing that I
was a genius," and "There was no reason for it
but I was, and he was not there was a reason for
it but he was not and that was the beginning of
the ending and we always had been together
and now we were never at all together. Little
by little we never met again."

Leo Stein's history is the all-too-common
one of early promise coupled with the inca-
pacity to fulfill it. He started and abandoned
many careers—art historian, scientist, painter,
and philosopher. He couldn't finish anything.
Some kind of hypercriticality kept him from

doing so. The writer Hutchins Hapgood, in his autobiography, *A Victorian in the Modern World* (1939), gives this telling description of Leo: "He was almost always mentally irritated. The slightest flaw, real or imaginary, in his companion's statements, caused in him intellectual indignation of the most intense kind. And there seemed to be something in him which took it for granted that anything said by anybody except himself needed immediate denial or at least substantial modification."

Leo was dismissive of Gertrude's writing—he believed she wrote the way she did because she couldn't write proper English—and he said something that Gertrude couldn't forgive. "He said it was not it it was I. If I was not there to be there with what I did then what I did would not be what it was," she writes in *Everybody's Autobiography.* "It did not trouble me," she adds. But in fact Leo's observation troubled her all her life and continues to trouble her posterity. "Perhaps after all they are right the Americans in being more interested in you than in the work you have done although they would not be interested in you if you had not

done the work you had done," she writes elsewhere in the book. If this can be said of any
celebrity artist, one must also say of Stein that
if she had not been as interested in herself as
she was she would not have written what she
wrote. She wrote almost exclusively, if not always openly, about her own experiences, and
of all writers she may be the one whose work
most cries out for the assistance of biography
in its interpretation. The "it" and the "I" are
never far apart.

Her "Melanctha" story in *Three Lives,* for
example, which for many years was celebrated
as some sort of wonderfully advanced study of
black life by a white writer (and, by today's
less innocent standard of what is advanced,
can only be called patronizing and uncom-
prehending), is based, not on Stein's experience of black life in America, but on a romance
between herself and a woman named May
Bookstaver, which began at Johns Hopkins and
broke her heart. "Melanctha" is Stein's second
stab at coming to terms with her heartbreak in
a piece of writing. The fake-black talk between

Gertrude Stein ca. 1900.

Melanctha and her lover Jeff is a new version
of the talk between the white women lovers in
Q.E.D., a novella Stein daringly wrote about
herself and Bookstaver in 1903 but didn't dare
publish in her lifetime. Similarly, the characters in Stein's massive novel *The Making of
Americans* derive from members of her own
family, though this time openly; indeed, Stein
often spoke of the members of her real and fictional families as if they were one. And even
the most hermetic of her writings are works
of submerged autobiography. The key of "I"
will not unlock the door to their meaning—
you need a crowbar for that—but will sometimes admit you to a kind of anteroom of
suggestion.

In 1914, Leo moved out of the rue de Fleurus and went to live in Florence. Some years
earlier, his job of making everything a pleasure
for his sister had been taken over by Alice Toklas (who moved in with Gertrude and Leo in
1909), and his departure had something of the
air of a shoe dropping. He and Gertrude divided the paintings and furniture and parted

forever. Gertrude's bruised feelings over Leo's stubborn refusal to acknowledge her genius were nothing compared to Leo's mortification and fury over his sister's success. As letters published after his death reveal, Leo was almost beside himself when *The Autobiography of Alice B. Toklas* came out to universal acclaim. He kept quizzing friends about their reaction, hoping to have them confirm his view of Gertrude as devoid of talent and of her admirers as "fatuous idiots who go to hear her silly twaddle." "I suppose you have read her autobiography," he wrote to the collector Albert Barnes in 1934, and went on: "The book seems to me a rather clever superstructure on a basis of impenetrable stupidity. Gertrude and I are just the contrary. She's basically stupid and I'm basically intelligent. But Gertrude's sort of massive self-admiration, and, in part, self-assurance, enabled her to build something rather effective on her foundations. I, on the other hand, through the upsetting, complicating and stultifying effects of a terrific neurosis, could build nothing substantial on my intelligence, which came through only in fragments and distorted bits."

It is generally agreed that without Alice Toklas, Stein might not have had the will to go on writing what for many years almost no one had any interest in reading. Stein's self-admiration and self-assurance needed to be fed, and Toklas appeared just in time to give them the nourishment Leo had withheld. Toklas recognized Stein's originality when Stein's self-confidence was at its lowest ebb. She banished doubt from Stein's artist's consciousness, as she would later banish the unworthy from Stein's salon. The division of household labor between the two women, with one doing everything and the other nothing, was another precondition for the flowering of Stein's genius. "It take a lot of time to be a genius, you have to sit around so much doing nothing, really doing nothing," Stein cheerfully reports in *Everybody's Autobiography*. Her literary enterprise was itself almost entirely work-free. Mabel Dodge's four-volume autobiography *Intimate Memories,* begun in 1924 (after her fourth marriage, when she became Mabel Dodge Luhan), gives a rare glimpse of Stein at her desk during the long visit she and Toklas made to the Villa Curonia in 1912. It was late at night and Stein was "writing automatically in a long weak handwriting—four or five lines to the page—letting it ooze up from deep down inside her, down onto the paper with the least possible physical effort; she would cover a few pages so and leave them there and go to bed, and in the morning Alice would gather them up." Stein never (or hardly ever) revised (a rare false start to *The Autobiography of Alice B. Toklas* exists among Stein's papers[1]), and in *Everybody's Autobiography* she said that she never wrote much more than half an hour a day (but added significantly, "To be sure all day and every day you are waiting around to write that half hour a day"). Stein didn't even type her work—she just oozed into her notebooks and Toklas did the rest.

The two women came from similar back-

grounds—second-generation Jewish-American
business families—and both lost their mothers
to cancer—Stein at the age of fourteen and
Toklas at twenty—but could not have been
more different in appearance and tempera-
ment. In *Intimate Memories*, the wickedly observant Mabel Dodge draws a vivid contrast
between them:

> Gertrude Stein was prodigious. Pounds and
> pounds and pounds piled up on her skeleton—
> not the billowing kind, but massive heavy fat.
> She wore some covering of corduroy or velvet
> and her crinkly hair was brushed back and
> twisted up high behind her jolly, intelligent
> face. . . . The year before Gertrude had lived
> in Fiesole—and she trudged down one hill
> and across town and up another to see us . . .
> and arrive[d] just sweating, her face par-
> boiled. And when she sat down, fanning her-
> self with her broad-brimmed hat with its
> wilted, dark brown ribbon, she exhaled a
> vivid steam all around her. When she got up
> she frankly used to pull her clothes off from
> where they stuck to her great legs. Yet with all
> this she was not at all repulsive. On the con-

trary, she was positively, richly attractive in her grand *ampleur*. She always seemed to like her own fat anyway and that usually helps other people to accept it. She had none of the funny embarrassments Anglo-Saxons have about flesh. She gloried in hers.

As for Toklas (to whom the bisexual Dodge was not drawn), she "was slight and dark, with beautiful gray eyes hung with black lashes—and she had a drooping, Jewish nose, and her eyelids drooped, and the corners of her red mouth and the lobes of her ears drooped under the black folded Hebraic hair, weighted down, as they were, with long heavy Oriental earrings. . . . She looked like Leah, out of the Old Testament, in her half-Oriental get-up—her blues and browns and oyster whites—her black hair—her barbaric chains and jewels—and her melancholy nose."

Dodge goes on to extend the comparison to the dinner table: Gertrude "loved beef and I used to like to see her sit down in front of five pounds of rare meat three inches thick and with strong wrists wielding knife and fork,

Alice B. Toklas in San Francisco, ca. 1902–3.
Photograph by Arnold Genthe.

finish it with gusto, while Alice ate a little slice daintily, like a cat." Soon after the visit, even though Dodge was a tireless promoter of Stein's work, Stein dropped her—and Dodge was convinced that Toklas was behind it. She cites the incident that she believes sealed her fate: "One day at lunch, Gertrude, sitting opposite me in Edwin's"—the absent Dodge's—"chair, sent me such a strong look over the table that it seemed to cut across the air to me in a band of electrified steel—a smile traveling across on it—powerful—Heavens! I remember it *now* so keenly! At that Alice arose hastily and ran out of the room on to the terrace." Stein went after her and returned saying that Toklas did not want her lunch. "She feels the heat today." "From that time on," Dodge writes, "Alice began to separate Gertrude and me—poco-poco." Ten years later Man Ray took a famous photograph of Stein and Toklas at 27 rue de Fleurus. They sit at opposite ends of a low table in front of a fireplace above which modernist works hang—Gertrude fat, handsome, comfortable, benevolent, Alice thin, plain, tense, sour. The photograph is a kind of parody

Gertrude Stein and Alice B. Toklas at 27 rue de Fleurus, 1922.
Photograph by Man Ray.

of the conventional society portrait of a hus-
band and wife at home—it shimmers with the
genre's sense of appearances being kept up and
things not being said. The word "lesbian" was
never publicly uttered by either of them about
their relationship—as it was the custom of the
day not to utter it. But the intensity of their
love is documented by Stein's erotic poems
(published after her death), by the memoirs of
contemporaries, and, in one extraordinary instance, by a piece of literary vandalism.

Toklas writes in her "Food in the Bugey"
chapter that "as the dreary dismal months
dragged on provisioning became easier and
more abundant, except for meat and butter,"
and, she adds, "More people came to see us,
even from Lyon, which is seventy miles distant. All in the *Resistance*, naturally." When I
read this in the fifties, the last sentence did not
cause me to smile knowingly, as it does today.
Then it went without saying that the people
Stein and Toklas saw during the war were the
good guys. But today I know that at least one

of the people who came to see Stein and Toklas at Culoz was not a good guy—indeed was one of the very worst guys, convicted of collaboration after the war and sentenced to a lifetime of hard labor.

He was Bernard Faÿ, a French university professor and writer, a gay man in his late forties, who came from a wealthy Royalist Catholic family, and whose right-wing connections led to his appointment in 1940 to head the Bibliothèque Nationale (replacing a Jew). Faÿ had been a close friend of Stein's since the early twenties—one of the few close friends with whom she didn't eventually quarrel and break. A photograph of him with Stein at Bilignin shows him to be a heavyset man with a mustache and glossy dark hair. Not visible in the photograph is his limp, the result of polio in childhood. His academic field was American history and culture (he had a graduate degree from Harvard, and among his books are biographies of Benjamin Franklin and George Washington, a work called *The Revolutionary Spirit in France and America,* and a study of American novelists), but he also cultivated the

avant-garde arts, and was a busy promoter of
Stein's writings in France (he translated *The
Autobiography of Alice B. Toklas* into French
and co-translated an abbreviated version of *The
Making of Americans*). In 1966—twenty years
after his conviction and sentencing, fifteen
years after he escaped from a prison hospital
and fled to Switzerland, and eight years after
he was pardoned by François Mitterrand—
Faÿ wrote a memoir called *Les précieux,* in
which he identified himself as Stein and Toklas's protector during the war. Part of his job
as head of the Bibliothèque, he writes, was to
act as adviser to Marshal Pétain, and once a
month he traveled from Paris to Vichy to con-
fer with the old man. During one of their meetings he found an opportunity to speak "about
Gertrude, her genius, the peril she was in, and,
more particularly, about the danger that she
might freeze to death in the coming winter."
He goes on:

> Before the meeting ended the Maréchal dic-
> tated a letter to the sous-prefect at Belley, en-
> trusting Gertrude Stein and Alice Toklas to

his care, and directing him to see to it that they had everything needed to keep warm during the winter, as well as ration coupons for meat and butter. I came to Vichy quite regularly, and I telephoned the sous-prefect to remind him of his instructions. During this horrible period of occupation, misery, and nascent civil war, my two friends lived a peaceful life. They didn't lack courage, they didn't lack intelligence, they didn't lack a sense of reality, and they didn't lack coal.

This account—along with a paragraph in a letter of 1955 from Faÿ to a Mr. Monahan giving a shortened version of the story—is the only known documentary evidence of Faÿ's intervention. Stein's and Toklas's biographers accept it as true. But Stein and Toklas never mentioned it in anything they wrote about their wartime experiences. Stein, in a letter written in March 1946, four months before her death, in which she defended Faÿ to the court that later convicted him, noted that he had saved her collection of paintings, but omitted to say that he had saved her life. Toklas, who lived until 1967, was similarly silent on the

subject. In nothing she wrote—including letters trying to get help for Faÿ in prison—did
Toklas acknowledge Faÿ's wartime protection.
Does this mean that Faÿ was lying about his
intervention in order to make himself look
good? Or was he telling the truth, and Stein
and Toklas kept silent because they couldn't
bring themselves to admit to the world that
they had been mixed up with a collaborator?

The answer to the question was given to me
by a professor of English named Edward M.
Burns. I had been much taken with an essay he
and another English professor, Ulla E. Dydo,
had written entitled "Gertrude Stein: September 1942 to September 1944" and published
as an appendix in their collection *The Letters
of Gertrude Stein and Thornton Wilder* (1996).
Burns and Dydo are distinguished Stein scholars. Burns had previously edited a two-volume
collection of the letters between Stein and
Carl Van Vechten (Van Vechten was the friend
whose slavish devotion to Stein practically
matched Toklas's; in his letters he called her
Baby Woojums—he was Papa Woojums and
Toklas was Mama Woojums), a book of Alice

Toklas's letters called *Staying on Alone,* and an illustrated book of Stein's writings on Picasso. Dydo, for her part, has produced *A Gertrude Stein Reader,* numerous papers on Stein published in scholarly journals, and a monumental critical study, *Gertrude Stein: The Language That Rises, 1923–1934.* But, in their essay on Stein in World War II, Burns and Dydo do not pull their punches in dealing with her problematic relationship to Faÿ, and they are equally stern about her perverse project, begun in late 1941 and evidently instigated by Faÿ, of translating a book of Pétain's speeches into English. Stein was not alone, of course, in her admiration for Pétain, the hero of Verdun. "What is difficult to understand, however, is how Stein continued with the project once edicts against Jews were issued and deportations begun," Burns and Dydo write, adding,

> It is as if in 1942–43 she was insulated from understanding what was happening. She had always been conservative, reactionary, and fearful of communism, and in the Spanish Civil War she had been anti-Loyalist. We do

not know to what extent she continued to
rely on Faÿ's judgment and what she understood of his political activities, his active anti-
Semitism, his hatred of Bolshevism, his collaboration. . . . In "Wars I Have Seen," filled
with astute observation of daily life, a reactionary tone sometimes creates discomfort.
What she understood about Faÿ and how
she saw the situation remains a troublesome
puzzle.

A page earlier, Dydo and Burns write of
Faÿ's escape from a prison hospital, on September 30, 1951, "with the help of friends."
One of these friends, they write, was Alice Toklas: "By means of the sale of one or more works
on paper by Picasso, Toklas helped to finance
the escape." I looked for the source of this
arresting information, but there was none—
neither in the text nor in a footnote. I telephoned one of the authors, and this led to a
series of meetings with Burns, Dydo, and another Stein scholar, William Rice, at Burns's
apartment on East Tenth Street in Manhattan.

Burns is a burly, affable, and loquacious
man in his early sixties, who entered the Stein

world when he was an undergraduate at Brooklyn College and took a course on American literature which Dydo was teaching there. Dydo's teaching of Stein, Burns said, was his first encounter with Stein's "real," or experimental, writing—as opposed to her accessible "audience" writing—and the beginning of the serious interest in Stein which became his life's work. Before writing the dissertation that was to become the Stein–Van Vechten volumes, Burns taught at the Charles Evans Hughes High School in Chelsea. (His own high school diploma, he told me, was jeopardized because he refused to sign the loyalty oath that was then a requirement of graduation.) He now teaches at William Paterson University, in New Jersey.

Dydo is a slender, elegant woman in her early eighties, who speaks with a European accent and has a tart manner that struggles with, and is defeated by, a deep underlying softheartedness. She grew up in Switzerland and came to this country in the late forties to get a master's degree at Bryn Mawr and then a doctorate at the University of Wisconsin. Her dissertation was on Allen Tate. "Tate interested me when I started," Dydo said at one of our meetings. "But he didn't continue to interest me. In the dissertation, I virtually said 'this work isn't interesting.' He was a traditionalist. And all that Southern business. I started reading Stein on my own at Wisconsin and that *was* interesting." After Wisconsin, Dydo taught for a few years at the Brearley School in Manhattan, then at Vassar, Brooklyn, and Bronx Community Colleges.

Rice, a tall, thin man in his seventies, with a sad and very kind face, is primarily a painter and actor, and therefore has a slightly different status in the trio. In the Thornton Wilder book and in Dydo's critical study, for example, he is given billing as "with William Rice." He entered the Stein world in 1980 when Burns hired him to do research and to type the manuscript of the Van Vechten book, and he remained to work with Burns and Dydo as a valued research assistant.

B urns and Dydo toil in different parts of the Stein vineyard. Burns has all the impulses of a biographer, though he lacks one crucial biographer's trait: the arrogant desire to impose a narrative on the stray bits and pieces of a life that wash up on the shores of biographical research. He is content to leave the bits and pieces as they are, and offer them in the footnotes and introductions and appendixes of the collections of letters he gathers. His appetite for research into Stein's life is almost unappeasable. He goes where no one else had thought of going, and comes back with trophies of great worth.

Dydo's concern, in contrast, is with Stein's texts, of which she is an extremely close reader, perhaps the closest reader Stein has ever had. She is a leading figure in the recent movement to accord Stein the status of a major modernist master and to read her work with sympathetic, rather than hostile, incomprehension. Indeed, as Jennifer Ashton, one of the new Stein critics, reports without irony in a paper entitled "Gertrude Stein for Anyone," published in the journal *ELH* in 1997, "Among more recent critical accounts that situate her as a precursor to postmodernism, unintelligibility—refigured as indeterminacy or indefinition—has become Stein's strongest virtue." Dydo's essays and her new book reflect an affinity for Stein's experimental writing that is so strong that it almost persuades the reader that he or she, too, can pick up any Stein text and read it with rapt delight. Dydo cherishes the anarchy of Stein's language. "By lifting words from the lockstep of standard usage, [Stein] stops us from unthinking association with things, ideas, and formulations," she writes in *Gertrude Stein: The Language That Rises*. "This process also does away with all the hierarchical trappings of grammar and with the distinction between important and unimportant words. Words cease to be signifiers and become objects in themselves." But Dydo has no illusions about the difficulty of Stein's writing. "Is Stein worth the effort to figure her out?" she pauses to ask in *The Language That Rises,* and allows the question to hover over its six hundred and fifty-nine pages.

Twenty years ago, Dydo set herself the Herculean task of establishing a true text for Stein's work. "Anybody who has ever copied or memorized a Stein piece knows that it is difficult to transcribe Stein accurately," Dydo writes in an essay called "How to Read Gertrude Stein," published in 1984 in the *Transactions of the Society for Textual Scholarship.* "Stein's syntax, grammar, and punctuation do not allow the typist or reader to rely unthinkingly on language habits when preparing or proofreading a Stein text." Accordingly, typists' and typesetters' errors that would leap out of texts written in ordinary English do not leap out of Stein's texts, and can be dislodged only through the painstaking comparison of printed text to manuscript. For more than two decades, Dydo has been reading printed texts against manuscripts and finding significant errors.

One of her most significant corrections was to the text of *Stanzas in Meditation,* an austerely impenetrable work, written in 1932— the same year, as it happens, that the beguilingly easy *Autobiography of Alice B. Toklas* was written— but not published until 1956, by Yale. The book-length *Stanzas,* characterized by one critic as "perhaps the dreariest long poem in the world,"[2] and by Dydo herself as "forbiddingly difficult," makes demands on the reader that only the most heroic of Steinians will not balk at. While comparing the manuscript and published versions of *Stanzas in Meditation,* Dydo came across something extremely odd. In the manuscript, she found that almost everywhere the auxiliary verb "may" appeared Stein had crossed it out and put in the word "can." For example, the lines "They may lightly send it away to say / That they will not change it if they may" were altered to "They can lightly send it away to say / That they will not change it if they can." In addition, when the month of May appeared it was crossed out and "day" or "today" was substituted. The revisions make no sense and are clear disimprovements. In some cases, the changes "twist the language to incomprehensible, even un-English phrasing," Dydo writes in *The Language That Rises,* as in "may be they shall be spared" changed to "can they shall be spared." The published text of the *Stanzas* was set from a typescript that reflected the revisions, and until Dydo examined the manuscript and a hitherto unexamined earlier typescript, no one knew that all the awkward "can"s in the poem had originally been "may"s and the "today"s and "day"s had been "May"s. Why had Stein subverted her work in this way? Dydo could not answer the question.

Then, in the summer of 1980, she had a dream that gave her the answer. Her painstaking work of comparison of manuscript and printed text was being done at the Beinecke Library at Yale, where most of Stein's manuscripts repose. Dydo would make periodic trips to New Haven and stay with a friend, but that summer there was no room at the friend's house, and Dydo had to make do with Spartan accommodations at a place called the Graduate Club. "It's the most depressing place there is," she told me. "It is a ramshackle old wood house. The boards creak. The rooms are not much more than monks' cells. There are sinks and narrow beds. There is no air conditioning. But it was close to the Beinecke and it was cheap. And that's where the dream came."

Dydo dreamed of an incident that Stein records in *The Autobiography of Alice B. Toklas,* in which she accidentally comes upon the manuscript of an early work of fiction. Stein does not identify the work, but we assume it is *Q.E.D.* "The funny thing about this short novel is that she completely forgot about it for many years," Stein writes in Toklas's voice, and goes on:

> She remembered herself beginning a little later writing the Three Lives but this first piece of writing was completely forgotten, she had never mentioned it to me, even when I first knew her. She must have forgotten about it almost immediately. This spring just two days before our leaving for the country she was looking for some manuscript . . . and she came across these two carefully written volumes of this completely forgotten first novel.

When Dydo awoke in her stifling room at the Graduate Club she knew in a flash that the word "may" in the *Stanzas* was connected to May Bookstaver, the thinly disguised love object of *Q.E.D.* In a paper published in 1985 in the *Chicago Review* entitled "*Stanzas in Meditation:* The Other Autobiography," Dydo spells

out the connection. She relates that when
Alice Toklas—who had known nothing about
the Stein-Bookstaver affair—read the "completely forgotten" novel,

> [she] was enraged. She destroyed—or made
> Gertrude destroy—May's letters, which had
> served as the basis for the early novel. She
> became, as she put it, "paranoid about the
> name May." That paranoia appears to be the
> key to the revisions of the text of *Stanzas.*
> Alice Toklas must have initiated the elimi-
> nation of the words *may* and *May* from the
> stanzas in the hope of purging the poems of
> Gertrude Stein of anything suggestive of May
> Bookstaver.

"How do you imagine the scene?" I asked
Dydo. She and Burns and Rice and I were sitting around a table in an alcove of Burns's living room, a light-filled space sparsely furnished
with modernist furniture, its walls crammed
with paintings, drawings, and photographs.
"Do you think Alice stood over Gertrude and
watched her change the 'may's to 'can's?"

"No," Dydo said.

"No," Rice said.

"It's far more punitive for Alice to say, 'You go there and you do it! You do it tonight! In your room!'" Dydo made her normally pleasant voice become a harsh bark.

"'Go to the corner and do it,'" Rice said.

"The manuscript tells a terrible story," Burns said. "The force with which these words are crossed out. The anger with which this was done. Some of the slashes go right through the paper."

"You almost expect to see blood," Rice said.

Stein's acceptance of the punishment inflicted on her poem by the infuriated Toklas is almost beyond understanding. How could a serious writer agree to such a crazy demand? But what does one know about other people's intimate lives? We know that jealousy can drive people to dire acts. We accept the idea of sadomasochism. Certain reports by contemporaries—and hints that Stein herself dropped—suggest that the "can"/"may" episode was not an isolated event but part of a regular repertoire of sadomasochistic games the couple played. The most striking of the reports is

Hemingway's. In his memoir *A Moveable Feast,*
he writes of an exchange he overheard between
Stein and Toklas whose violence so unnerved
him that it effectively ended his friendship
with Stein. Hemingway tells of coming to see
Stein at 27 rue de Fleurus and being told to
wait by a maid, who brings him a glass of eau-
de-vie. He continues:

> The colorless alcohol felt good on my tongue
> and it was still in my mouth when I heard
> someone speaking to Miss Stein as I had never
> heard one person speak to another; never,
> anywhere, ever.
> Then Miss Stein's voice came pleading and
> begging, saying, "Don't, pussy. Don't. Don't,
> please don't. I'll do anything, pussy, but
> please don't do it. Please don't. Please don't,
> pussy."

What Hemingway wrote about Stein and Toklas in *The Moveable Feast* has been regarded
with skepticism. It is thought to be his revenge
for Stein's putting him down in *The Autobiography of Alice B. Toklas* ("Gertrude Stein and
Sherwood Anderson are very funny on the sub-

ject of Hemingway. . . . They both agreed that they have a weakness for Hemingway because he is such a good pupil. He is a rotten pupil, I protested. You don't understand, they both said, it is so flattering to have a pupil who does it without understanding it," and "He looks like a modern and he smells of the museums"). But in the light of what pussy did to Stein's poem Hemingway's account no longer seems so suspect.

It was in the course of a trip to Europe in 1968 to collect letters for *Staying on Alone* that Burns stumbled on the story of the Faÿ escape that made its way into the appendix of the Thornton Wilder book. On the same trip, he visited Belley and spoke to Maurice Sivan, who had been the *sous-préfet* in Faÿ's story (misspelled Sivain in Stein's story of the terrifying moment at the lawyers)—and who confirmed it in every detail. So that question was answered. The answer to the question about Toklas and the escape was more tortuous. "Four people told me about it," Burns said.

"First there were the Knapiks—Harold and Virginia—who became good friends of Alice's after Gertrude's death. They were Americans living in Paris. Harold was an extraordinary cook, and Alice put several of his recipes into her cookbook."

When Burns uttered the name Harold Knapik I could see the page in the cookbook on which Knapik's recipe for Szegely Goulash appeared, and I could even recite his prefatory comment: "This is the goulash that I mentioned. It is not bad but its origin on the Hungarian plain is reflected a little insistently." The remark stayed with me—it is the sort of thing Clovis Sangrail might have said about goulash—and endeared Knapik to me. And now he was about to emerge as a real and no doubt very different person from the one I had imagined. I had already had to revise my idea of another contributor to the cookbook (Toklas gathered these contributions into a chapter called "Recipes from Friends"). This was Fania Marinoff, whose Lamb Curry for Six is one of the most stained of all the pages in my copy of the book. In my imagination Fania was a Jew-

ish matriarch who lived on West End Avenue
and never got out of her brunch coat. But from
photographs in *The Letters of Gertrude Stein
and Carl Van Vechten,* I have had to accept the
fact that Fania—the game second wife of the
gay Carl Van Vechten—was a beautiful and
slender young Russian actress.

Burns paused for dramatic effect and said,
"The Knapiks are dead now, so it's all right for
me to say this: they were CIA agents. Harold's
cover—he was a musician—was that he was
working on a book on counterpoint; Virginia
worked at the American embassy." My idea of
Knapik remained intact. Of course he was a
CIA agent.

Burns went on, "The Knapiks told me
they knew of Alice's involvement in the escape
but said that a certain Madame Azam was
the person I should talk to, because she knew
most about it. Madam Azam, née Cohen, was
a rich, cultivated elderly Frenchwoman who
lived in Paris. She was a Jewish convert to
Catholicism and a good friend of Faÿ's and,
eventually, of Alice's. She said that Faÿ walked
with her on the street in Paris when she had to

wear a yellow star. When I interviewed Madame Azam she said, 'Alice and I were influential in arranging for Bernard's escape. We helped with the money.' She told me that the people who got him out were dressed as nuns. Then she gave me an introduction to Faÿ and I went to see him."

"What did you make of him?" I asked Burns. "What was he like?"

"He was perfectly charming. I met him in a beautiful Paris apartment that belonged to his brother. I started to try to struggle along in French and he said, no, it did him good to speak in English. He was a little wary of me at first and then gradually began to trust me. You know how it is when you're able to give bits and pieces of information that you have. He eventually became very warm and gave me some of his books. But I remember feeling uneasy and having the sense that this was not a very nice person. You have to understand that I was staying with Kahnweiler,[3] who said, 'I know you're doing this for your work on Gertrude, but he's a perfectly detestable man.'"

As Burns talked, Ulla Dydo and Bill Rice

sipped beer and listened attentively, as though they, too, were hearing the story for the first time. Burns went on with his narrative. "When I went to see Faÿ, I played two roles. I was there for information and to get letters from him for the book. I felt a certain excitement— here was a man who knew Gertrude and about whom Gertrude had written. I'd ask him a question about Gertrude and the answer would be something Gertrude had said to him. It was like touching the shoes of a fisherman. But then there was my Jewishness—thank you very much. It's a situation where you feel unclean. You know that under normal circumstances you would not sit in the same room with this person."[4]

A few weeks earlier, I had spoken on the telephone with Gilbert Harrison, who wrote an introduction to the Burns collection of Toklas's letters. (I had known him in the late fifties when he was editor of the *New Republic*.) He, too, told me of a meeting he had had with Faÿ in Paris. It took place in 1937. Harrison, then a very young man, intended to call on Stein and Toklas, as many very young men did in those days. Three years earlier, he had attended one of Stein's American lectures (in Pasadena), had stopped her in the lobby afterward, and had talked with her for an hour. But now, on presenting himself at 27 rue de Fleurus, he found no one home. He telephoned Faÿ (whom he had met in America through Stein), who told him that the women were in Bilignin, obligingly offered to arrange an invitation, and, in the meanwhile, asked him to lunch with him and his sister. "It was a very good and very elegant lunch and the sister was so elegant herself that she hardly condescended to speak to us," Harrison said. He added: "One remark of Faÿ's I will never forget. 'Why don't you stay in Paris?' he said. 'I can arrange for you to get a scholarship, since you're not a Jew.'" I asked Harrison (who *is* a Jew) what he said. "I was absolutely silent," he replied.

In an introduction Faÿ wrote for the abbreviated English edition of *The Making of Americans,* he is (as in everything he wrote about and to Stein) obsequious to a degree that would be simply laughable were it not inflected by our knowledge of his sinister collaboration.

I have seen her many times in town surrounded with her "Picassos" and her friends,
always picturesque, always amusing, or in the
country surrounded by flowers, dogs and her
peasant neighbors which seem as much hers
as flowers or dogs, because when she speaks of
them and when she speaks to them, her voice
and her understanding give them a realness
that human beings only reach when they just
get out of a dream to face for a very short time
the true sharp life of early morning. . . . I have
found Gertrude Stein always the same and
always new. Every time I came near her it
seemed to me that life and things became precise, that light was shining frankly on everything and with her I had the pleasure of talking as if words had a meaning and as if the
meaning of everything, words and things,
were pleasant.

Stein, on her side, wrote about Faÿ less
inanely, but with fondness, in both *The Autobiography of Alice B. Toklas* and *Everybody's Autobiography.* After Carl Van Vechten, he was her
staunchest supporter and helper. In *The Autobiography of Alice B. Toklas,* she writes, obviously as a kind of inside joke, of a first meeting

with Faÿ that was unsuccessful: "Bernard Faÿ
was not at all what Gertrude Stein expected
and he and she had nothing in particular to say
to each other." But presently "Gertrude Stein
and Bernard Faÿ met again and this time they
had a great deal to say to each other. Gertrude
Stein found the contact with his mind stimu-
lating and comforting. They were slowly coming to be friends." Stein cannot resist mischievously adding:

> I remember once coming into the room and
> hearing Bernard Faÿ say that the three people
> of first rate importance that he had met in his
> life were Picasso, Gertrude Stein and André
> Gide and Gertrude Stein inquired quite simply,
> that is quite right but why include Gide. A
> year or so later in referring to this conversa-
> tion he said to her, and I am not sure you were
> not right.

Hemingway wrote bitterly—and he was
not the only ex-friend to make this point—
that "in the three or four years that we were
good friends I cannot remember Gertrude
Stein ever speaking well of any writer who had

not written favorably about her work or done something to advance her career except for Ronald Firbank and, later, Scott Fitzgerald." Faÿ zealously performed both services. He frequently taught and lectured in America; thus, when Stein went on her American lecture tour in 1934 he was able to pave the way for her at many universities. He also rehearsed her lectures with her—in fact, he taught her the technique of lecturing. Most important, he promoted Stein's work in France through his translations and flowery tributes.

An almost palpable odor of oily flattery emanates from the collection of his letters to Stein at the Beinecke. Over the twenty years of the friendship, the stationery and the handwriting change, but the obsequiousness never wavers. Even in the final letters, written from prison on stationery quite different from the luxe black-bordered writing paper on which Faÿ wrote his early notes, the habit of sucking-up remains unbroken—as in the following, written on October 15, 1945: "I feel and enjoy from my cell your affection and your vitality. As soon as you can, send me some of the things

you have written recently. I am terribly eager
to see it. 'American literature' is the great fad
now all over France and particularly here. I
have been talking a lot about American writers
and most of all about you here with a lot of
people."

What was in it for Faÿ? What drew the
Royalist anti-Semite to the Jewess in funny
clothes? In his chapter on Stein in *Les précieux*
Faÿ writes thus of his first encounter with her
in 1924: "She was quite corpulent and vigorous
and resembled a 2nd century Roman emperor
who might have had Jewish blood. She had her
hair cut very short. Her fine face shone with
authority and intelligence and she was wearing
a blouse with a variegated embroidered vest
and a short khaki skirt and khaki stockings
and yellow leather sandals." Anti-Semites, as is
well known, often actually have best friends
who are Jews; it comes with the territory. It
gives them a thrill. Stein would have been a
perfect object for the obligatory transgressive
fantasy of friendship with an exceptional Chosen Person. In *Les précieux* Stein's Jewishness
looms large. Faÿ writes of walking with her at

Bilignin and talking about "the most daring of subjects." "She liked to talk to me about God," he writes, and continues,

> "Now Bernard," she said to me, "You must understand that Jews have never taken the afterlife into account. In the Bible God's job is to improve life on earth, to protect and guide his people, but there's never a question of an afterlife or eternity." I forbore to bring up my own knowledge of the Bible, which was more direct than hers, and contented myself with replying, "A material, earthly, practical God is an idol. Only a spiritual God who is superior to men and their limited notion of time and space and life and death merits the adoration which the Jews, wise and worthy people, could never have given him if they had not felt in his presence the terror that the other world, the Beyond inspires."

Readers of *Everybody's Autobiography* may recall Stein's account of her rueful early realization that "there was no mention of everlasting" in the Hebrew Scriptures. "When I was about eight," she writes, "I was surprised to know that in the Old Testament there was

Gertrude Stein and Bernard Faÿ at Bilignin,
in the 1930s.

nothing about a future life or eternity. I read it
to see and there was nothing there. There was a
God of course and he spoke but there was nothing about eternity." Whether the conversation
Faÿ records actually took place or whether he
invented it after re-reading *Everybody's Autobiography* can be known only to the denizens of
the Beyond. Faÿ, apparently unable to relin-
quish his Jewish theme, goes on to say that
once, when he had said something clever about
Picasso, Stein "turned to me and looked me
straight in the eye and said, 'Be honest, Bernard, admit it. You are much too intelligent
not to be Jewish.'" Of course, it's possible that
Stein uttered this cliché, but somehow one
doubts it. She prided herself on her originality
and unpredictability. She would sometimes
say extraordinarily silly things, but they were
her own silly things, never the silly things other
people had said.

In *Wars I Have Seen* there is a telling moment when Stein—in the course of absurdly
remarking that Hitler wants to destroy Germany because he is an Austrian and thus har-
bors a deep unconscious hatred of Germany—

pauses to say that when she first delivered
herself of this aperçu at a dinner party in Paris
in 1935, "they all thought that I was only trying to be bright but not at all it is true." Stein's
habitual attempt to be bright is a defining
characteristic of her life and her art. She
seemed to shine when she walked into a room,
and the work, even at its most hermetic, pos-
sesses a glitter that keeps one reading long past
the time when it is normal to stop reading a
text that makes no sense. The showing off that
is the youngest child's prerogative and man-
date was forged by the grown Stein into a for-
midable social and artistic tool.

Although Thornton Wilder's letters to Stein
are as complimentary as Faÿ's, they are in
no way off-putting; the compliments have an
ironic edge that only brings the genuineness
of his affection for her into relief. Thus when
(in a footnote) Dydo and Burns quote a letter
Wilder wrote to Alexander Woollcott in September 1933, in which he takes a hard look at
Stein's evasiveness about her Jewishness, we
do not feel that he is being two-faced. Rather,
we feel he is cutting to the chase:

I suppose you've read the Alice B. Toklas. Well, Gertrude Stein is a fine, big serene girl, is she? beyond prejudice,—beyond being touched by the world's good or bad opinion? THEN: why does she never mention that she or Miss Toklas are Jewesses? And why in the bundle of pages which were all that I could endure of that 1000 page work ("the first great book written in the future") "The Making of Americans" does she not mention that the family she is analyzing in such detail is a Jewish family. And why in fabricating a fictitious name for her family does she contrive one that only faintly might be Jewish.

It's Henry Adams' wife, again. It's possible to make books of a certain fascination if you scrupulously leave out the essential.

In *Wars I Have Seen* Stein continues to leave out the essential. She just can't seem to bring herself to say that she and Toklas are Jewish. But the Nazis' persecution of the Jews is clearly on her mind, and the book is full of indirect allusions to it. She writes of the Dreyfus case and anti-Semitism, mentions Jewish refugees, and tells a story that could well be a disguised story about herself:

There is this about a Jewish woman, a Parisienne, well known in the Paris world. She and her family took refuge in Chambery when the persecutions against the Jews began in Paris. And then later, when there was no southern zone, all the Jews were supposed to have the fact put on their carte d'identité and their food card, she went to the prefecture to do so and the official whom she saw looked at her severely. Madame he said, have you any proof with you that you are a Jewess, why no she said, well he said if you have no actual proof that you are a Jewess why do you come and bother me, why she said I beg your pardon, no he said I am not interested unless you can prove you are a Jewess, good day he said and she left. It was she who told the story. Most of the French officials were like that really like that.

The discussion of the Dreyfus case and anti-Semitism is abruptly interrupted by a strange passage that would seem to belong to one of the experimental works rather than to the book in hand, which is written in (more or less) ordinary English. The passage goes:

He can read acasias, hands and faces. Acasias

are for the goat, and the goat gives milk, very
necessary these days and hands and faces are
hands and faces, and dreams when one is
dancing and falls asleep are real, and all this
has this to do with anti-semitism that it
is true and not real and real and not true.

Claudia Roth Pierpont, in an essay on Stein
in her book *Passionate Minds: Women Rewriting
the World,* wittily holds up this "senseless bab-
ble" as an instance of Stein's "long-standing
way of handling all serious unpleasantness: pretend it isn't there and then tumble into nonsense or baby talk, so that perhaps it will be
persuaded that you are not there, either—or,
at least, that you are not a reasonable target."
I felt there was truth in Pierpont's observation,
but wondered whether her impatience with
Stein, like my own, wasn't based on a too early
diagnosis of senselessness. Knowing of Dydo's
dedication to making what she calls "Gertrude-
sense" of Stein's unintelligible texts, at my next
meeting with the trio of Stein scholars, I read
aloud the passage and asked Dydo if she knew
what acasias had to do with anti-Semitism.

"I have no idea," she said.

I made a lame joke: "Maybe you could dream about it."

"I can't dream on command," Dydo answered, deadpan. "But I'll see what I can do."

And over the next week she sent me e-mails about elements of the passage, identifying the acacia tree as the Old Testament burning bush and the goat as a sacrificial animal, and pointing out that the passage is led up to by several pages of musings about the imprisonment of innocent people—such as Oscar Wilde, as well as Alfred Dreyfus. I myself began to look and look again at the passage, and was rewarded for my persistence with an illumination. I realized that the phrase "dreams when one is dancing and falls asleep" referred to a dance marathon in Chicago to which Stein and Toklas had been taken during the American lecture tour. In these horrifying Depression entertainments impoverished young couples competed for prize money, dancing, sometimes for weeks, until they dropped. In *Everybody's Autobiography*, Stein describes the marathon: "Here there was nothing neither waking nor sleeping. They

were young ones and they were moving as their
bodies were drooping. They had been six weeks
without sleeping and some no longer had another one with them they were moving and
drooping alone but when there were two of
them one was more clinging than moving."
(Stein also wrote to Carl Van Vechten about the
marathon: "they are like shades modern shades
out of Dante and they move so strangely and
they lead each other about one asleep completely and the other almost, it is the most un-
earthly and most beautiful movements I have
ever seen.") Now, in June 1943—Stein an-
nounces the progressive months of the war as if
keeping a diary—she identifies with the sleep-
walking dancers. "It is true and not real and
real and not true." A few pages earlier, after
narrating the story of the *sous-préfet*'s warning
to flee to Switzerland or be put in a concentration camp, she concluded: "But what was so
curious in the whole affair was its unreality."
She also wrote of the incident, "It took us some
weeks to get over it, but we finally did." But it
took her from February to June to bring herself to tell the story, and surely she had not got

over it. *Wars I Have Seen* is permeated with Stein's anxiety. Two years earlier, Stein had channeled her dread into a novel called *Mrs. Reynolds* about a couple of ordinary people who are living in the oppressive shadow of two sinister men called Angel Harper and Joseph Lane, meant to represent Hitler and Stalin. Richard Bridgman, in his classic study *Gertrude Stein in Pieces* (1970), dryly remarked that "'Mrs. Reynolds' cannot be advanced as a pleasurable reading experience." For most people, it is an impossible reading experience; the book is written in Stein's most cruelly boring experimental style. "There is nothing historical about this book except the state of mind," Stein wrote in an epilogue. *Wars I Have Seen* records both history and a state of mind, and there is nothing quite like it in the literature of war or, for that matter, in Stein's writings.

It is a work of realism struggling against itself. *The Autobiography of Alice B. Toklas* reflected Stein's deep, almost purring satisfaction with its form. *Wars I Have Seen* reflects Stein's ambivalence toward the form she has chosen or that, perhaps, has chosen her. In the

early pages of the book there is an almost au-
dible clash of wills between Stein's divided
selves. We can almost hear the one self say, No,
I will not narrate, and the other say, Please try.
In *The Autobiography of Alice B. Toklas,* Stein
boasted that her story "Melanctha" "was the
first definite step away from the nineteenth
century and into the twentieth century in literature." For forty years Stein has been working as a twentieth-century modernist innova-
tor. But now she is obliged to consider the
possibility that the nineteenth century did not
end when she and everyone else thought it did,
but is only ending now, with the arrival of bar-
barism. "Realism was the last thing the nineteenth century did completely. Anybody can
understand that there is no point in being realistic about here and now . . . it is not the nineteenth but the twentieth century, there is no
realism now, life is not real it is not earnest, it is
strange which is an entirely different matter."
And yet, paradoxically, something tells Stein
that there is great point in being realistic now,
that life is indeed real and earnest and that she
must try to rouse herself. "The horrors the

fears everybody's fears the helplessness of everybody's fears, so different from other wars makes this war like Shakespeare's plays." Stein knows better than to try to write like Shakespeare, but she also senses that the occasion demands that she not try to write like herself, either. Modernist experimentalism will not express what she wants (and doesn't want) to express.

The journalist Eric Sevareid was one of the first Americans to reach Culoz after the liberation of Paris. In his book *Not So Wild a Dream* (1946), he writes of his meeting with Stein, in early September 1944, and reports that she told him that "with all the difficulties, the isolation from lifelong friends, these had been the happiest years of her life." Readers of *Wars I Have Seen* will not believe her, of course. But if they have read Stein's other autobiographies, they will not doubt the accuracy of Sevareid's reporting. It was a point of pride with Stein never to appear unhappy. In *Everybody's Autobiography*, she writes: "About an

unhappy childhood well I never had an unhappy anything. What is the use of having an
unhappy anything" and: "If you write about
yourself or anybody it sounds as if you were
very unhappy and very bitter but generally
speaking everybody living has a fairly cheerful
time in living. . . . Any life you look at seems
unhappy but any life lived is fairly cheerful,
and whatever happens it goes on being so."
Whatever happens it goes on being so may be
the most oblivious of the oblivious things Stein
kept permitting herself to say. Perhaps a girl
whose mother dies of cancer when she is fourteen, after years of suffering, needs to develop
calluses. What probably began as a defensive
pose became an ingrained characteristic: Stein's
preternatural cheerfulness may be her most
outstanding personality trait. In *Wars I Have
Seen* she is obliged to drop the pose and to acknowledge her profound unhappiness. It is
surely no accident that in using the term "medieval" to describe the dark time in which she
is living—"medieval means that life and place
and the crops you plant and your wife and children, all are uncertain. They can be driven

away or taken away, or burned away, of left behind, that is what it is to be medieval"—she as-
sociates the term with "the dark and dreadful
days of adolescence, in which predominated
the fear of death." Stein, writing *Wars I Have
Seen* at an age when fear of death is rather better founded than at fourteen (she is approach-
ing seventy and will die of stomach cancer in
1946, at seventy-two), pauses to muse that "if
everybody did not die the earth would be all
covered over and I, I as I, could not have come
to be and try as much as I can try not to be I,
nevertheless, I would mind that so much, as
much as anything, so then why not die, and yet
and again not a thing, not a thing to be liking,
not a thing." But it is the war's visible threats,
rather than mortality's veiled ones, that are
Stein's subject and the object of her terror.
Over and over, she writes of her fearfulness and
helplessness in the face of the evil she cannot
bring herself to imagine and yet on some level
has understood.

By the time Stein met with Sevareid, she
had more than regained her cheerfulness, which
may have clouded her memory of the five-year-

long ordeal she had undergone. The "plot" of *Wars I Have Seen*, if we can use that term to describe its narrative trajectory, is the change from Stein's hysterical despair alternating with rationalization, to hope alternating with fear, to unmitigated ecstatic joy when the Liberation comes.

During the period of despair, she writes: "Now when here in France when we all thought the young men were safe they are now all being taken away well it is like that, Shakespeare was right it is all just like that." The deportation of young Frenchmen to forced labor in Germany is one of her persistent themes. These deportations were, of course, of anguishing concern to the people in the village—to the parents and siblings of the young men and to the young men themselves—but one cannot help conjecturing that they also represented to Stein the specter of what could happen to her and Toklas. When Stein reports the absurd advice she gave to a group of young men about to be shipped off to Germany—she tells them to "study" the Germans, "learn their language and get to know their literature, think of yourselves as a tourist not as a prisoner"—one can only think that she was imagining her way into her own possible predicament, and whistling in the dark as she did so. The betrayals and denunciations she hears about on the long daily walks she takes with her dog in search of extra food have a similar personal resonance. She and Toklas are at the mercy of the villagers who could at any moment betray them as Americans and Jews. But the villagers never do—they are evidently as much in love with Stein as were the soldiers in World War I who cranked her car and changed her tires.

Stein's growing willingness to keep her attention fixed on the actual occurs in tandem with—and is surely influenced by—the turning of the tide against the Germans. By the fall of 1943, it was beginning to be apparent that an Allied victory was only a matter of time. Life no longer seems unreal to Stein. In September 1943, she sees things with great clarity:

> The one thing that everybody wants is to be free . . . not to be managed, threatened, directed, restrained, obliged, fearful, admin-

istered, they want none of these things they
all want to feel free, the word discipline, and
forbidden and investigated and imprisoned
brings horror and fear into all hearts, they do
not want to be afraid not more than is necessary in the ordinary business of living where
one has to earn one's living and has to fear
want and disease and death. . . . The only thing
that any one wants now is to be free, to be let
alone, to live their life as they can, but not to
be watched, controlled and scared, no no, not.

Stein's account of the winter of 1943–
44—the fifth winter of the war, "just one winter too much"—renders the exhaustion of
waiting for the end and also the fear of the
dangerous wounded beast the Germans have
become. ("Is it worse to be scared than to be
bored, that is the question," she remarks at
one point.) She reports the stories told to her
by the people she meets on her walks: arrests,
deportations, interrogations, killings are their
usual subject. A moment of comic relief is offered by a woman who tells her about another
woman in the town of Bourg who had just
given birth to six puppy dogs. "Not possible, I

said, but yes she said . . . in times like these
women do console themselves with dogs and
this does happen, of course the dogs don't sur-
vive they are kept in museums, but it does
happen, not really I said, oh yes, she said, in
Bourg they once had it happen to a nun, and
when the doctor went to see her the dog would
not let him come near her." Another walk
yields a scene of melancholy poetry: Stein has
walked high up a mountain and then, descend-
ing as it is getting dark and beginning to snow
and sleet, she is passed by small groups of
men—the young men who have hidden out in
the mountains rather than be sent to Germany,
and are coming down from their freezing lairs
to have a meal and spend the night with their
families.

When the winter finally ends, and the in-
vasion seems imminent, the word "Maquis"
begins to appear more and more frequently in
Stein's text. The narrative now pushes forward
like a stream no longer choked by fallen trees
and debris. The Normandy landing takes place,
and the Germans stop acting like conquer-
ors and begin to display their cravenness and

poshlust. The villagers openly make fun of
them. But when, ten days after the landing,
Stein and Toklas receive a letter from the Swiss
consul in Lyon "who has charge of american
interests" inviting them to apply for repatria-
tion, "we giggled we said that is optimism.
Naturally American authorities not really realizing what it is to live in an occupied country
ask you to put down your religion your property and its value, as if anybody would as long
as the Germans are in the country and in a position to take letters and read them if they
want to. The American authorities say they are
in a hurry for these facts but I imagine that all
Americans will feel the same better keep quiet
until the Germans are gone just naturally play
possum just as long as one can. Just that."
"Put down your religion" is as close as Stein
will come to the point. The rueful consterna-
tion of Dydo, Burns, and Rice and the sharp
criticism Stein has received from less kindly
disposed writers in regard to her apparent in-
difference to the fate of the Jews are not blunted
by *Wars I Have Seen.* While she covertly identifies with the persecuted Jews, overtly she dis-

tances herself from them. There are even passages that border on the anti-Semitic, such as
her bizarre aperçu that the Jewish "instinct for
publicity" is "the real basis of the persecution
of the chosen people."

As the book progresses, there is less and
less of this kind of stuff. When Stein finally
finds her true voice, when she no longer needs
to struggle against the here and now by re-
treating into silliness, the book becomes almost unbearably exciting and moving. On the
day Paris is liberated:

> it was just like fourth of July in my youth in
> the San Joaquin valley, it was just as hot and
> we all went today that Paris was freed to put
> flowers on the soldiers monument, it had al-
> ready been draped with flags and the maquis
> marched down the main street of Culoz, and
> then everybody stood at attention and sang
> the Marseillaise. . . . I like to call them maquis,
> that was what they were, when every moment
> was a danger, they had to receive arms they
> had to transport them and they had to hide
> them and they had to do sabotage and all the
> time a very considerable part of their country-

men did not at all believe in them, and there
they were workmen, station masters, civil servants, tailors, barbers, anything, nobody knew
but they naturally, and some of them looked
pretty tired but my everybody was happy,
everybody had the flag on their shoulders. . . .
Paris was taken at noon and by eight o'clock
all France was putting wreaths on their sol-
dier's monument because of course every village has that, honneur aux maquis, and they
say that Americans are at Aix-les-Bains only
twenty five kilometers away.

When Stein meets her first Americans,
"How we talked and how we patted each other
in the good American way, and I had to know
where they came from and where they were
going and where they were born. In the last
war we had come across our first American soldiers and it had been nice but nothing like
this. . . . We went to look at their car the jeep,
and I had expected it to be much smaller but it
was quite big and they said did I want a ride
and I said you bet I wanted a ride."

Stein invites two of the American soldiers to
her house. "Here were the first Americans ac-

tually in the house with us, impossible to believe that only three weeks before the Germans had been in the village still and feeling themselves masters, it was wonderful. . . . That is all I can say about it wonderful, and I said you are going to sleep in beds where German officers slept six weeks ago, wonderful my gracious perfectly wonderful. How we talked that night . . . and my were we happy, we were, completely and truly happy and completely and entirely worn out with emotion."

"The writing in *Wars I Have Seen* is magnificent," Ed Burns said with a mild air of surprise during another meeting at his house. He said he had re-read the book in preparation for our now habitual talks, and had forgotten, or perhaps had not realized, how remarkable it was. Dydo and Rice echoed his surprised admiration. All three prefer Stein's "real" writing to the "audience" writing, and when I confessed—as I am often obliged to—that the "real" writing is not congenial to me, they looked at me pityingly.

"Well, you're honest," Dydo said kindly on one of these occasions. On another, while talking about the Thornton Wilder–Gertrude Stein book, I said in passing that I liked *Our Town*, and Dydo gave me a dark look. "Is it too sentimental for you?" I asked. "Ugh," she said, and shuddered. At these times I feel like someone who has ordered a cheeseburger at Lutèce.

Burns had just returned from Paris bearing major trophies of research. Before his trip, he had asked if there were anything he could do for me in Paris, and I had asked if he knew someone—a graduate student maybe—who might be able to pry loose from the authorities a copy of the transcript of Bernard Faÿ's trial. I knew from contemporary newspaper accounts that Faÿ was convicted of persecuting French Freemasons, but I wanted to know more precisely what he had done, and whether he had received a just verdict. A French authority on the Vichy period named Pierre Assouline, to whom Burns had referred me earlier, and with whom I had spoken on the phone, said he believed the record of the trial was sealed, but gave me the name of the gov-

ernment office I might apply to for declassifi-
cation, along with the address of a specialized
library that would have information about
Faÿ. Burns was vague about finding a graduate
student, but took down the name and address
of the government office and the library. A few
days after his arrival in Paris, Burns sent me
and Dydo the first of a series of increasingly excited e-mails about Faÿ's war record, which—
his researcher's instincts aroused—he had decided to investigate himself. A visit to the specialized library had led Burns to a man named
Lucien Sabah, a police official in the French
Ministry of the Interior, who had written a
book entitled *Une police politique de Vichy: Le
service des sociétés secrètes,* in which Faÿ's persecution of Freemasons is reported in damning
detail. Burns also learned of a boyfriend of
Faÿ's named Geuydan de Roussel, who was a
Gestapo agent, and who kept a journal of his
own and Faÿ's activities for the Germans between 1940 and 1944. The flatly factual journal
(which Sabah has edited and published in a
small edition), establishing Faÿ's connection to
the Gestapo, proved even more damning than

the polemical Sabah book. Burns had told me
that when he interviewed Faÿ, he had said,
"No one died because of me. I was not respon-
sible for anyone's death."

But now Burns learned that Faÿ was re-
sponsible for many deaths. The prosecutor at
Faÿ's trial (Sabah had seen the transcript) pre-
sented documents showing that, because of
Faÿ's zeal in naming names by way of execut-
ing Pétain's 1940 order banning secret soci-
eties, a hundred and seventy thousand Masons
had files created for them, sixty thousand were
investigated, six thousand were imprisoned,
nine hundred and ninety were deported, and
five hundred and forty were shot or died in
camps. (Burns and Dydo, in their appendix
essay, put the Nazi persecution of Freemasons
into a larger context: "Fearful of religious tol-
eration, political compromise, loyalty to local
authority and the power of secrecy, totalitar-
ian states—from Nazi Germany and Austria,
Fascist Italy, Spain, and Portugal to the Soviet
Union and Communist China—banned Free-
masonry.") In August 1941, Faÿ had written to
Stein about his wartime job: "My own life is

very full and very fruitful. *I do a lot of things that are not always pleasant,* but are always interesting. . . . The Marshall is very nice to me and they say he will appoint me a minister soon" (unpublished letter at the Beinecke, italics mine). Exactly how unpleasant these things were can now be understood.

"I am beginning to know more than I want to about this detestable man," Burns wrote from Paris. "I doubt, however, that Gertrude knew any of this. In Faÿ she probably saw only the old friend who had helped her in so many ways, including getting the confidence to make the lecture tour." Alice Toklas clearly didn't know either. For years before the escape, she had worked on getting Faÿ released from prison, in much the same way she and Stein had worked on getting the lieutenant out of the dream house in Bilignin. But the influential people (in France and America) she tried to interest in her cause wouldn't touch it. (One of these, Donald Sutherland, a professor of classics at the University of Colorado, whom Toklas approached about finding Faÿ a teaching job in America in the case of his release, wrote in a 1968 essay entitled "The Conversion of Alice B. Toklas": "I never met Bernard Faÿ, but I knew several of his friends, who, with the exception of Alice, loathed him. He appeared to have as many personal as political enemies, being possessed of a nasty tongue.") Perhaps Stein might have achieved the impossible; Toklas couldn't. Only when the Catholic Church thought it safe to intervene—Burns believes that the escape and university appointment in Fribourg were largely engineered by the Church—was the "miracle" (as Toklas called it) worked.

In one of Toklas's letters of supplication (this one to a prominent Chicago society woman named Bobsy Goodspeed), she wrote that Stein's feeling for Faÿ made it mandatory for her to work to free him. It was "a sacred trust." In a letter of November 1946 to Carl Van Vechten, she permitted herself this: "He has been in Fresnes prison since the liberation accused of hating communists (who doesn't) acting against the masons (who wouldn't in France) hating the English (the large majority of Frenchmen do) hating the Jews (is he alone?)." Unknown to Toklas, when Sutherland had asked Van Vechten "what I was supposed to make of Bernard Faÿ, when I thought he should have been shot outright but Alice was of an entirely different opinion," Van Vechten had replied, "I can't endure Bernard." And, unknown to Bobsy Goodspeed, Faÿ had described her to Stein, in a letter of 1934, as "a good-looking, silly-clever Evanston lady, wife of the foremost trustee and lover of the wife of the president of the University of Chicago."

When Eric Sevareid met Stein in Culoz in 1944, this was not his first encounter with her. He had called on her in Paris in 1937 and was, as he writes in *Not So Wild a Dream*, "deeply impressed by the finest flow of talk I had ever listened to with the possible exception of that from Schnabel, the pianist." Sevareid continues,

> She has a remarkably lucid and germinal mind and disguises a profound understanding by a simplicity of rapidly flowing speech that mis-

leads the casual listener. . . . In written form
her words seem bizarre and difficult to follow,
but when she herself reads them aloud it is all
perfectly lucid, natural, and exact. She had
just then finished her own version of Faust.
She walked heavily up and down her study in
front of her dark Picassos and read the script
aloud to me, carried away by her own words
and breaking off into ringing laughter which
so overcame her at times that she would stop
to wipe her eyes. She was a warm and wonderful person.

However, when it came to politics, Sevareid
thought Stein less wonderful:

She could not think politically at all. Thus she
assured me:

"Hitler will never really go to war. He is not
the dangerous one. You see, he is the German
romanticist. He wants the illusion of victory
and power, the glory and glamour of it, but he
could not stand the blood and fighting involved in getting it. No, Mussolini—there's
the dangerous man, for he is an Italian realist.
He won't stop at anything." She did not understand Fascism; she did not understand that

the moods and imperatives of great mass
movements are far stronger and more important than the individuals involved in them.
She knew persons, but not people.

But by the time of the writing of *Wars I Have
Seen*, Stein seems finally to have got it. "I used
not to understand but I am beginning to now,"
she writes near the end of the book. She has
just reported a row she had had on the street
with one of "the decayed aristocrats who are
always hoping that a new regime will give them
a chance and [who] are the most furious of
all against the defeat of the Germans." A few
pages earlier, she had written of "some firm re-
actionaries who are convinced that all maquis
are terrorists, we have some charming neighbors who are like that and it worries me because after all people get angry and things
might happen to them and we are very fond of
them." These "charming neighbors" must have
been the members of the Croix de Feu, a perni-
cious right-wing organization founded by vet-
erans of World War I, with whose views Stein
had previously agreed, and among whom she

had many friends in the Belley area. When, in 1937, her friend W. G. Rogers wrote to object to her position on the Spanish Civil War, she wrote back from Belley: "I interested all our french friends here who are all Croix de feu by telling them how you felt about Spain" and went on to write page after page of reactionary piffle. But now she has corrected course. "When political issues were clarified by the eventual line-up of powers in the second World War," Rogers writes in his memoir, "it was as plain to Miss Stein as it was to all the rest of us that there were no two ways about it, it had to be democracy, it couldn't be totalitarianism." Earlier in the memoir, writing of the seeds of American corn he annually sent Stein and Toklas for planting in the Bilignin garden, he notes that during the Spanish Civil War "I had told her I hoped none of my honest Loyalist corn would be served to any of her friends of the wrong political persuasion." In *Everybody's Autobiography* Stein recalls the rebuke and impudently writes, "we had corn the Kiddie"— Stein's pet name for Rogers—"who sends it to us says now we must not give it to any fascists

but why not if the fascists like it, and we liked
the fascists, so I said please send us unpolitical
corn." But six years later, writing to Rogers
from Vichy France, Stein humbly acknowledges
her error. Of the corn she is planting in her garden she now writes: "And it is allied corn you
may be sure."

After the arrival of the Americans in Culoz,
"I began to have what you might call a
posthumous fear," Stein writes in her epilogue
to *Wars I Have Seen.* She reflects that during
the occupation the demands of daily life had
largely kept fear at bay, but "now somehow
with the American soldiers questions and hearing what had been happening to others, of
course one knew it but now one had time to feel
it and so I was quite frightened." *What had
been happening to others.* Again, Stein is almost
but not quite saying it. Toklas never did. Although Stein sometimes referred to Toklas as
"my little jew" and "my little hebrew" in the
erotic poetry she wrote about her "marriage"
to Toklas, Toklas herself never mentioned her

(or Stein's) Jewishness. Throughout the twenty years of her widowhood she behaved as if it simply didn't exist. How Stein would have situated herself in the post-Auschwitz world, had she lived, we cannot know, of course. From the evidence of her chronic contrariness, we may assume that pussy's way would not have been her own.

PART TWO

I think it is safe to say that most well-read people in the English-speaking world have not read *The Making of Americans*. The book (in its only available edition) is nine hundred and twenty-five pages long and is set in small dense type, forty-four lines to the page. It is believed to be a modernist master-piece, but is not felt to be a necessary reading experience. It is more a monument than a text, a heroic achievement of writing, a near-impossible feat of reading.

For years, even writers on Stein felt absolved from reading all, if not any, of the forbidding volume. Edmund Wilson, in his chapter on Stein in *Axel's Castle* (1931), writes, almost with pride, certainly without shame, that "I have not read [*The Making of Americans*] all through, and I do not know whether it is possible to do so." He goes on, "With sentences so regularly rhythmical, so needlessly prolix, so many times repeated and ending so often in present participles, the reader is all too soon in a state, not to follow the slow becoming of life, but simply to fall asleep." When Marianne Moore reviewed the book for the *Dial,* in 1926, she was less candid than Wilson about her inability to read it all through, but it is obvious from the review that she didn't get much past the first fifty pages.

Stein's own friends felt under no pressure to read the book. "Of course I have not had time to do anything more than dip into many parts of it," the painter Harry Phelan Gibb unapologetically wrote to her in October 1925, feeling that it was enough to say that "only a few pages tells you when there is something remarkable and great." Sherwood Anderson wrote with similar aplomb—and language—

"I had saved your book for the quiet of the country and have been dipping into it." The friends who did more than dip into the book, were at a loss to talk about it. "To me, now, it is a little like the Book of Genesis," Carl Van Vechten, who later became Stein's literary executor, babbled after reading an early section. "There is something Biblical about you, Gertrude. Certainly there is something Biblical about you."

In recent years, as interest in Stein has grown in the American academy, the shirking of the reading of *The Making of Americans* has fallen out of favor. Critics who write about the book are expected to read it. Richard Bridgman, one of the earliest non-shirkers, gives an admirable précis of the text in *Gertrude Stein in Pieces;* but he does not underestimate the book's difficulty. "[It] gives the impression of someone learning how to drive," he writes (as if from the passenger seat), and goes on, "Periodically there are smooth stretches, but these are interrupted by bumps, lurches, wild wrenchings of the wheel, and sudden brakings. All the while the driver can be heard muttering re-

minders and encouragements to herself, im-
precations, and cries of alarm."

For a long time I put off reading *The Making of Americans*. Every time I picked up
the book, I put it down again. It was too heavy
and thick and the type was too small and
dense. I finally solved the problem of the
book's weight and bulk by taking a kitchen
knife and cutting it into six sections. The book
thus became portable and (so to speak) read-
able. As I read, I realized that in carving up the
book I had unwittingly made a physical fact of
its stylistic and thematic inchoateness. It is a
book that is actually a number of books. It is
called a novel, but in reality it is a series of long
meditations on, among other things, the author's refusal (and inability) to write a novel.

The meditations begin only after an attempt is made to write a conventional nine-
teenth-century novel. The heroine is a young
woman named Julia Dehning, the eldest daugh-
ter of a rich, second-generation American im-
migrant family, who is about to make a disas-

trous marriage to a bounder. Stein writes in
the guise of an outspoken omniscient narrator,
an "I" who likes to interject her own tart views,
but still accepts standard novelistic norms. On
page 33, she suddenly breaks loose from these
norms:

> Bear it in your mind my reader, but truly I
> never feel it that there ever can be for me any
> such a creature, no it is this scribbled and
> dirty and lined paper that is really to be to
> me always my receiver,—but anyhow reader,
> bear it in your mind—will there be for me ever
> any such a creature—what I have said always
> before to you, that this that I write down a
> little each day here on my scraps of paper for
> you is not just an ordinary kind of novel with
> a plot and conversations to amuse you, but a
> record of a decent family's progress respectably
> lived by us and our fathers and our mothers,
> and our grand-fathers, and grandmothers,
> and this is by me carefully a little each day to
> be written down here. . . . And so listen while
> I tell you all about us, and wait while I hasten
> slowly forwards, and love, please, this history
> of this decent family's progress.

This passage is remarkable for many reasons, most of all, perhaps, for Stein's repeated mention of the paper on which she writes. Like Maurice Denis's provocative dictum of 1890—"Remember, a picture, before being a battle horse or a nude, or some anecdote, is essentially a flat surface covered with colors assembled in a certain order"—Stein's invocation of her scribbled and dirty and lined paper comes out of the new climate, called modernism, that French painters are being warmed by and that she is one of the first literary artists to feel. Her book is going to concern itself with the conditions of its making in the way the paintings of Cézanne and Picasso and Matisse concern themselves with the conditions of theirs. Hovering over the work is an image of a woman sitting at a desk stubbornly performing her daily task of covering blank pieces of paper with words; and this woman is the real heroine of the book. Julia Dehning disappears and only reappears three hundred pages later; other characters come and go; but the writer figure remains. The jolts and lurches of her engagement with writing are the book's plot. The

Gertrude Stein at 27 rue de Fleurus, 1913.
Photograph by Alvin Langdon Coburn.

reader never really cares what happens to the characters, but becomes increasingly curious about what their author is up to.

Stein now turns to the family of the bounder, the Hersland family, which is based on her own family. She adopts a new style. She has already written *Three Lives*, and the new style has some resemblance to the earlier work in its abstractness but has none of its concision. It is as if Stein had made a rule for herself that she must allow every subject to exhaust itself before letting go of it. Nothing is ever said once. It is always said many times with slight variations creeping in as they do in repeats in music. Thus we read over and over about the mother Fanny Hersland, the "little unimportant mother," who "was lost among them and mostly they forgot about her, now she died away among them and they never thought about her, sometimes they would be good to her, mostly for them she had no existence in her and then she died away and the gentle scared little woman was all that they ever after remembered of her." As we know, Stein's own mother had died of cancer when

Stein was fourteen. In *Everybody's Autobiography* Stein writes, "When my mother died she had been ill a long time and had not been able to move around and so when she died we had all already had the habit of doing without her." She adds: "I have told all about her in *The Making of Americans* but that is a story and after all what is the use of its being a story. If it is real enough what is the use of it being a story." And, "What is the use of remembering anything. There is none." But remembering had great use for Stein in the writing of *The Making of Americans*. The passages about the "unimportant" mother are some of the finest writing in the book. In Stein's oblique telling of her story of unacceptable loss, she achieves an extraordinary level of expressiveness. The refrain about the mother's unimportance has the effect, of course, of implying the opposite. Stein breaks through the hard shell of her child's self-protectiveness, and allows herself to mourn her mother. She does so in a characteristically perverse way. She writes, at great length, not about her grief but about the servants who did not need to harden themselves

119

against the dying woman and who gave her the
sense of being needed that "the angry father
and the three big resentful children" refused
her. "Those who always after remember about
her were the servants, the governesses, the
dependents who had been around her, they
always were a real life to her, they were the important feeling in her, they always remembered about her, they had felt the real important being to herself inside her."

When Stein wrote the Fanny Hersland section, she was still at an early stage in her journey; her book was to turn into something that
no one could have predicted—something so
monstrously peculiar that although it is possible to finish, it is impossible to sum up. Each
critic must be content to grapple with one or
two boughs of this redwood of literature. One
generalization that can be made, however, is
that it is a dark, death-ridden work and that
the Fanny Hersland section establishes the
atmosphere that is to pervade it to the end.
After Stein completed the book, in 1911, this
atmosphere lifts, and never again descends on
her work. Even *Wars I Have Seen* has the con-

fident playfulness that we associate with the figure of Gertrude Stein. *The Making of Americans* was a work that Stein evidently had to get out of her system—almost like a person having to vomit—before she could become Gertrude Stein as we know her. A great outpouring of grief and anger and sorrow and doubt had to take place before the certainties and jollities of the mature writer could come into being. The cool ease of the mature Stein was preceded by writing of hysterical, sometimes almost mad intensity. As *The Making of Americans* progresses it resembles less and less a novel and more and more a morass into which writer and reader are sinking together.

It is well to remember while reading this strangest of strange books that Stein did not start out as a writer. From Radcliffe, on the advice of her teacher William James, she went to medical school at Johns Hopkins in preparation for a career in psychology. In her last year, she flunked several courses and declined to take them over in order to graduate.

In *The Autobiography of Alice B. Toklas*, Stein recalls the end of her medical career with amused relief. "Her very close friend Marion Walker pleaded with her, she said, but Gertrude Gertrude remember the cause of women, and Gertrude Stein said, you don't know what it is to be bored." However, the end of Stein's medical career did not mark the end of her interest in psychology; if anything, that interest increased. She and Leo, with growing obsessiveness, first in Baltimore and later in Paris, took apart their friends' characters and then—for their own good, of course—told them what was the matter with them.

This moralistic hobby became the basis of the program of character analysis that takes over *The Making of Americans* at around page 290 and puts an end to any resemblance whatever the work may have to a regular novel. The "decent family's progress" comes to a halt. Now, in addition to—and for many pages instead of—rendering the Dehnings and the Herslands Stein writes about unnamed individuals who exemplify the various kinds of people there are in the world—whom she proposes to classify in the way Linnaeus classified plants. According to Stein's system of classification, everyone in the world is either "dependent independent" or "independent dependent": "Independent dependent being is when the natural way of fighting is attacking, dependent independent being is when the natural way of fighting is resisting." Stein makes her determination of what people are by listening to them repeat themselves. At the outset, she exults in the almost magical power of understanding that has come to her.

> They are all of them repeating and I hear it. I love it and I tell it. I love it and now I will write it. This is now a history of my love of it. I hear it and I love it and I write it. They repeat it. They live it and I see it and I hear it. They live it and I hear it and I see it and I love it and now and always I will write it. . . . This is then a beginning of the way of knowing everything in everyone, of knowing the complete history of each one who ever is or was or will be living.

This is then a little description of the winning
of so much wisdom.

But Stein's triumph is short-lived. "Loving re-
peating" is not enough. "There are so many
complicated kinds of these two kinds of them,"
she realizes,

> so many ways of mixing, disguising, compli-
> cated using of their natures in many of them,
> so complicated that mostly it is confusing to
> me who know it of them that there are these
> kinds of them and always more and more I
> know it of them and always it is confusing for
> sometimes a resisting one spends most of liv-
> ing in attacking, an attacking one spends most
> of the living in resisting, sometimes some one
> is mostly all attacking and just at the bottom
> there is a contradiction of the whole nature of
> them, there are so many complications then
> in all this that I am knowing, it is all a very dif-
> ficult thing to be really understanding.

Stein's increasing awareness of the unhelpful-
ness of her system of character analysis oc-
cupies her for the next hundred pages. She

struggles against her growing realization that actually she doesn't understand people at all: "Perhaps no one ever gets a complete history of any one. This is very discouraging thinking. I am very sad now in this feeling. Always, hearing something, gives to some a sad feeling of realizing everything they have not been hearing and that they are not knowing and perhaps they can never have really in them the complete history of anyone, no one ever can have in them the complete history of anyone." And: "I am all unhappy in this writing. . . . I am nervous and driving and unhappy in it." In her desperation, she begins to admit strange reifications into her system:

> Resisting being in men and women . . . is like a substance and in some it is as I was saying solid and sensitive all through it to stimulation, in some almost wooden, in some muddy and engulfing, in some thin almost like gruel, in some solid in some parts and in other parts all liquid, in some with holes like air holes in it, in some a thin layer of it, in some hardened and cracked all through it.

And:

> I am thinking of attacking being not as an
> earthy kind of substance but as a pulpy not
> dust not dirt but a more mixed up substance,
> it can be slimy, gelatinous, gluey, white opaquy
> kind of thing and it can be white and vibrant
> and clear and heated and this is all not very
> clear to me.

Her images grow ever more repellent:

> I am always feeling each kind of them as a
> substance darker, lighter, thinner, thicker,
> muddier, clearer, smoother, lumpier, granu-
> larer, mixeder, simpler like every kind there is
> of earth or anything and always I am feeling in
> each one of them their kind of stuff as much
> in them, as little in them, as all of a piece in
> them, as lumps in them held together some-
> times by parts of the same sometimes by
> other kinds of stuff in them. . . . Some are al-
> ways whole though the being in them is all a
> mushy mass with a skin to hold them in and so
> make one.

The anti-novel seems to be turning into a kind of nervous breakdown. The author has regressed to a state where she evidently cannot differentiate writing from shitting:

> Sometimes it comes out of me I am filled full of knowing and it bursts out from me, sometimes it comes very slowly from me, sometimes it comes sharply from me, sometimes it comes out of me to amuse me, sometimes it comes out of me as a way of doing a duty for me, sometimes it comes brilliantly out of me, sometimes it comes as a way of playing by me . . . sometimes it comes very repeatingly, sometimes very willingly out of me, sometimes not very willingly, always then it comes out of me.

Perhaps no other book makes it so plain to the reader that it is being written over time, and that, like life, it is inconsistent and changeable. Just when it looks as if Stein has taken permanent leave of her senses and will never stop gibbering about the mushy sausage-like things she has replaced her characters with, she snaps out of it and returns to the Herslands. She tells a story from the early childhood of Martha Hersland, a rather dispirited girl who "was never really very interesting to anyone," and who is based on her young self.

This one was a very little one then and she was running and she was in the street and it was a muddy one and she had an umbrella that she was dragging and she was crying. "I will throw the umbrella in the mud," she was saying, she was very little then, she was just beginning her schooling, "I will throw the umbrella in the mud," she said and no one was near her and she was dragging the umbrella and bitterness possessed her, "I will throw the umbrella in the mud" she was saying and nobody heard her, the others had run ahead to get home and they had left her, "I will throw the umbrella in the mud," and there was desperate anger in her; "I have throwed the umbrella in the mud" burst from her, she had thrown the umbrella in the mud and that was the end of it all in her. She had thrown the umbrella in the mud and no one heard her as it burst from her. "I have throwed the um-

brella in the mud," and that was the end of it
all in her.

This story has been much quoted—by Stein
herself, among others—and it has the ring of a
seminal memory. But no sooner does Stein tell
it than she repudiates it. "It is very hard telling
from any incident in any one's living what kind
of being they have in them," she writes, and
goes on: "It is very hard to know of any one the
being in them from one or two things they have
been doing that some one is telling about them,
from many things even that they have been
doing and that one knows of them. Knowing
real being in men and women is a very slow pro-
ceeding and always more and more this is very
certain."

Stein's own occasional reversions to conventional narration of the "one or two things
they have been doing that some one is telling
about them" sort give the book a movement
like that of a train that now and then comes up
to speed but mostly crawls along because of
track work. Stein keeps returning to the project it appears she has abandoned—that of

writing fiction—and then berates herself for doing it badly. "Sometimes I am almost despairing," she writes. "I know the being in Miss Dounor that I am beginning describing, I know the being in Miss Charles that I am soon going to be beginning describing, I know the being in Mrs. Redfern, I have been describing the being in that one. I know the being in each one of these three of them and I am almost despairing for *I am doubting if I am knowing it poignantly enough* to be really knowing it, to be really knowing the being in any one of the three of them. Always now I am despairing" (italics mine).

Tolstoy and Dickens and Jane Austen knew it poignantly enough. Stein, realizing that she is not equipped to create fictional characters, and yet believing herself to be a literary genius, stubbornly persists in her task of filling pieces of paper every day with her earnest and remarkable thoughts. Presently she makes another daunting discovery: "I have not any dramatic imagination for action in them, I only can know about action in them from knowing action they have been doing any of them. . . .

I cannot ever construct action for them to be doing."

In other words, she cannot invent. She can only write about what has actually happened to people she knows. And yet she is hardly doing what other writers do who lack dramatic imagination—journalists, biographers, memoirists. If her characters do not resemble the characters of fiction (it is amusing to think of Anna Karenina as a mass of gritty dried stuff held together by a skin. Or Emma Woodhouse as something white and gelatinous), neither do they resemble the characters of biography, memoir, and reportage. The characters in *The Making of Americans* resemble shades. You never see them. Stein makes sure you know almost nothing concrete about them, sometimes not even their sex. This is truly a new way of writing a novel, a novel where the author withholds the characters from the reader. Stein regards her characters as if from a great distance and, at the same time, seems, in her desperate eagerness to understand them, almost to be taking them into her mouth and tasting them. Only the narrator remains a full-blooded

131

person, for whom one feels increasing sympathy and a sort of stunned admiration.

What the stakes are for the narrator—why her strange taxonomy is of such desperate importance to her—becomes clearer as the book progresses. It is some sort of defense against death. Death weaves in and out of the narrative and takes it over in the end, in the solemn and mysterious section about the troubled second Hersland son, David, who obscurely wills his own early death. "Dead is dead," the narrator grimly observes midway through the book. But some pages later she writes of the comfort she derives from the idea that every individual is a type or kind. "This is a pleasant feeling, this is comforting to me just now when I am thinking of every one always growing older and then dying, now when I am thinking about each one being sometime a sick one each one being sometime a dead one." She goes on in her incantatory way, "I am having a pleasant completely completed feeling and always then it is a comfortable and calming thing this being certain that each one is one of a kind of them in men and women and that there are always very many of each kind existing . . . that each one sometime is to be a dead one is then not discouraging."

The narrator does not explain why her fear of death is allayed by the idea of types. We can only conjecture that it is less threatening for her to contemplate the extinction of "one of a kind" than of an irreplaceable, unique individual. But, whatever she means, her pleasant confident feeling is, as always, short-lived. "I am in desolation and my eyes are large with needing weeping and I have a flush from feverish feeling," she writes. "I tell you, I cannot bear it this thing that I cannot be realizing experiencing in each one being living." Her typology is no longer sufficient. Now she wants to have intimate and complete knowledge of every individual in the world and, of course, "I know I will not, and I am one knowing being a dead one and not being a living one, I who am not believing that I will be realizing each one's experiencing." The narrator doesn't spell out the connection between her fear of death and her realization that she is not omniscient. Again, we can only conjecture. She herself is

aware of the incommunicability of her mad-
deningly complex thoughts:

> I mean, I mean and that is not what I mean. I
> mean that not any one is saying what they are
> meaning, I mean that I am feeling something,
> I mean that I mean something and I mean
> that not any one is thinking, is feeling, is say-
> ing, is certain of that thing, i mean that not
> any one can be saying, thinking, feeling, not any
> one can be certain of that thing, i mean I am
> not certain of that thing, i am not ever saying,
> thinking, feeling, being certain of this thing, I
> mean, I mean, I know what I mean.

The Making of Americans is a text of magisterial disorder. That its unruliness was not
foreign to Stein is illustrated by a letter of 1897
from a fellow Harvard student named Leon
Solomon, to whom she had sent a scientific article. "You ought to be ashamed of yourself for
the careless manner in which you have written
it up," Solomon wrote, and went on:

> The trouble with the article as it stands is that
> one has to hunt around too much to find the

important points,—it is as bewildering as a detailed map of a large country on a small scale. What it needs is relief, perspective. You must make perfectly clear to yourself just what you regard as the essentials of the work, and devote all your energies to bringing them out. As it is one is apt to miss the essentials in irrelevant or at least less important details. . . . Don't be afraid of leaving things out. . . . In short don't emulate our friends the Germans, but be a little French.

Stein could become a little French only after being very German. "Nothing must ever be thrown out," she writes in one of her riffs on the maddening difficulty of seeing "a whole one" through the ever-murkier lens of her apparatus of classification. She refuses to see things clearly that can only be seen darkly. She would rather groan and beat her breast than impose a false order on disorderly complexity.

It takes a long time to read *The Making of Americans*. The language Stein writes in (after cutting herself loose from the conventional language of the opening Dehning section) is not the transparent language through which we enter stories, forgetting we are reading. We never forget we are reading while reading *The Making of Americans.* In a recent talk about the book John Ashbery said that after years of pretending he had read it (he could never get past page 30), he finally did and was glad. He added, "I would like to do it again, although I've already read it about three or four times since I had to read every sentence, I think, at least that many times." Stein's language draws attention to itself the way the brushstrokes of modernist paintings do. It forces re-reading. (I did not have Ashbery's fortitude and read the book only twice.)

Stein's vocabulary is small and monotonous. When she uses a new word it is like the entrance of a new character. It is thrilling. "Every word I am ever using in writing has for me very existing being," she writes. "Using a word I have not yet been using in my writing is to me very difficult and a peculiar feeling. . . . There are only a few words and with these mostly always I am writing that have for me completely entirely existing being, in talking I use many more of them of words I am not living but talking is another thing, in talking one can be saying mostly anything, often then I am using many words I never could be using in writing."

Stein seems to be transcribing rather than transforming thought as she writes, making a kind of literal translation of what is going on in her mind. The alacrity with which she catches her thoughts before they turn into stale standard expressions may be the most singular of her accomplishments. Her influence on twentieth-century writing is nebulous. No school of Stein ever came into being. But every writer who lingers over Stein's sentences is apt to feel a little stab of shame over the heedless predictability of his own.

On November 24, 1952, Alice Toklas wrote to Carl Van Vechten about the death of Basket II, the white poodle she and Gertrude Stein had acquired in 1938 to replace the recently deceased Basket I. "His going has stunned me—for some time I have realized how much I depended upon him and so it is the beginning of living for the rest of my days without anyone who is dependent upon me for anything," Toklas told Van Vechten, leaving unspoken an obvious parallel: the Toklas-Stein relationship. Stein had been the extra-smart, unruly pet whom Toklas took exemplary care of and upon whose dependence she depended. The hole that Stein's death left in Toklas's life was never filled. There was no Gertrude II. After Stein's death in 1946, Toklas took on some canine characteristics of her own. She tended the shrine of Stein's literary and personal legend with the devotion of the dog at the master's grave. She would snarl if anyone came too close to the monument.

In her letter to Van Vechten, Toklas did not dwell on the death of the dog, but quickly went on to write of developments in "the work with Katz," a project that was making increasing claims on her time and attention. A few weeks before Basket succumbed, Leon Katz, a thirty-three-year-old Columbia University doctoral candidate, who was preparing a dissertation on Stein's early writings, appeared at Toklas's apartment on the rue Christine (Toklas and Stein had moved there from the rue de Fleurus in 1938), like a proleptic gift of distraction from the gods. He dangled before her a remarkable scholar's treasure. In 1948, while working in the Stein archive at the Yale library, Katz had come across a cache of small notebooks filled with Stein's penciled scrawls: notes she had made between 1902 and 1911 while composing *The Making of Americans* and other early texts, and had never shown to anyone, even to Toklas (except for a few pages she had once let her read). The notebooks had come to Yale in 1938, in two parcels wrapped in brown paper, thrown in among the manuscripts Stein had sent over on the urging of Thornton Wilder, who saw that war was coming. Stein had apparently forgotten what was in the brown paper parcels, and Toklas had assumed they contained manuscripts. After the bundles were unwrapped, no one at Yale took particular notice of their contents.

Katz found the notes of electrifying interest. He saw them as a kind of Rosetta stone with which to decode *The Making of Americans*, and received permission from Van Vechten and from Donald Gallup, the curator of the Stein archive at Yale, to make a transcript of them; further, he was granted exclusive rights to publish them. He came to Toklas to guide him through the maze of the notes, scrawled by Stein at odd moments and hedged by the obscurity as well as shimmering with the authenticity of writing not intended for any eye but one's own. He had hundreds of questions to ask Toklas about the dozens of people who appeared in them; he had already interviewed a large number of Stein's still-living friends and relatives.

Toklas liked young men, the way Stein had, though she didn't always like the same young men. She had never liked Hemingway, for example. But this young man was "ever so nice—gentle and sensitive and amiable," as she described him to Van Vechten in the letter of November 24. Not that she immediately trusted him. Toklas, then seventy-five, was the least

credulous of old women. With Stein she had
played the role of the suspicious protector of
a vulnerable, openhearted child. (In her letters to Van Vechten, she referred to Stein as
"Baby.") But Toklas's defenses—like those of
the old woman in *The Aspern Papers*—could be
penetrated. Katz's charm obviously affected
her, as did his assurance that he had no immediate plans for publication. The edition of
the notes she would be assisting him prepare
would indefinitely repose in the Yale library
as a "sealed manuscript." ("It is to be hoped
that Katz's work will not be open to even stu-
dents for a considerable period," she wrote to
Van Vechten.) But perhaps most decisive in
Toklas's willingness to answer Katz's questions
was her own curiosity about the notebooks.
"You now see that eagerness to see the notes of
which Gertrude showed me only a small part—
led me on," she wrote to the scholar Donald
Sutherland on January 8, 1953. "Nothing but
really nothing could have stopped me."

Thus from November 1952 to February
1953, eight hours a day, four days a week, Tok-

las received Katz in her sitting room and pored over the notes with him, "line by line—word by word," as he interrogated her about Stein in the early years of her writing career. (They worked with a four-hundred-page typed transcript that Katz had made.) At first, before her suspicions were put completely to rest, Toklas was evasive when Katz asked questions that "bothered me," as she recalled to Sutherland. "One answered by refusing to answer very much like an FBI investigation." But once the matter of publication was settled, "my answers and asides," as she put it to Van Vechten, "became of an indiscretion that will please you." The notes themselves were, as Toklas excitedly realized, a font of indiscretion—and self-revelation. Toklas wrote to Sutherland: "[Gertrude]—alone with herself and the originals of her characters and portraits—could be of a frankness that makes indiscretion appear pale. Carl and Gallup hastily looked through the notes one afternoon after Katz had copied them and . . . were surprised to learn how greatly Gertrude had exposed not only people she knew . . . but herself."

In his dissertation (accepted by Columbia in 1963), called "The First Making of 'The Making of Americans': A Study Based on Gertrude Stein's Notebooks and Early Versions of Her Novel (1902–1908)," Katz predicted that after the publication of Stein's notebooks, "the biographical legend formed around her name, largely perpetrated by her own autobiographical writing, will undergo major revisions of emphasis." However, Katz did not go back on his word to Toklas and rush the notebooks into print. Sixty-one years after Stein's death and forty years after Toklas's, Katz has yet to publish the notes, although Yale gave him permission to do so, and Liveright Publishing signed a contract with him to produce an edition in which his annotations and Toklas's commentaries would appear, to be published in 1974, Stein's centenary year. The original handwritten notebooks and Katz's typewritten transcript may now be read at the Beinecke Library, at Yale, but Katz's notes of his interviews with Toklas in Paris remain locked in his possession—no scholar has ever seen them. This is not to say that Katz kept

Toklas's indiscretions to himself. His dissertation is filled with them—indeed, is, in certain respects, poised on them.

Although "The First Making of 'The Making of Americans'" never came out as a printed book, in the world of Stein criticism and scholarship it has become a kind of cult classic. (It is available in typescript form from ProQuest Information and Learning, in Ann Arbor.) References to it appear in all serious writing on Stein since the sixties. Virgil Thomson, reviewing a group of books on Stein in the *New York Review of Books* in 1971, articulates the feeling of excitement that an encounter with the dissertation engenders. He writes of "a new pinnacle, high and possibly dangerous to inexpert navigation, like a partly exposed iceberg, known as the Katz manuscript." Thomson had in fact read only a version of some of the dissertation's most interesting pages, published as a preface to a collection of Stein writings called *Fernhurst, Q.E.D., and Other Early Writings.* But he had read enough to grasp the dissertation's distinction, noting that it "peers out from odd footnotes" in the other books under review "like a sudden searchlight."

Thomson's association of the dissertation both with a searchlight and with an iceberg has a rightness to it. As well as illuminating an obscure period of Stein's life, the thesis also threatens the image of Stein that Toklas had been at such pains to preserve. "Much of the Stein that is concealed in the autobiographies is revealed only too plainly and unpleasantly in the notebooks," Katz writes, as he prepares, with the assistance of Toklas's indiscretions, and the bad-mouthings of Stein's relatives and friends, to render the young Stein as a confused and morose young woman, recovering from an unhappy lesbian love affair, and dazedly attempting to write. Toklas would surely have been mortified by Katz's portrait of Stein, but there is no reason to think that she read the dissertation. In 1963, she was eighty-six years old and could hardly see. She died in 1967, in apparent ignorance of Katz's betrayal.

Katz challenges the *Autobiography*'s picture of Stein's early life in Paris as the lovely adventure of an American who, as Stein writes, "happened to be in the heart of an art movement of which the outside world at that time knew nothing." Katz bluntly points out that, on the contrary, "far from living on the horizon of current French art," Stein lived in a kind of ghetto of American relatives and friends, whose French acquaintance was limited almost exclusively to servants, tradesmen, and concierges. "From the notebooks and from her letters of the first months in Paris—in fact of her first four years there," Katz writes, "—it is clear that Stein underwent a period of the most relentless despair, surrender of ambition, and psychological disorientation. She became passive, cynical; she was moved to do nothing." He adds,

> Later, times such as these were lost to her in a mist of self-congratulation, daily pleasure and indeed of a newly reinforced egomania that had begun to overtake her after she finished "The Making of Americans" and recognized frankly and with a kind of astonished joy the

overwhelming scope of her achievements.
"Slowly I was knowing that I was a genius."
And with the years, that knowledge was increasingly borne in on her and manifested
itself in uglier and uglier ways. She did not recall the dull, stubbornly persistent miseries of
her first months in Paris.

The notebooks are the record of a peevish
soul trying to break out of a trap. Their
author is an irritable and hypercritical young
woman, living with a brother she is beginning to hate and among a set of American
women she thinks she is trying to understand
but whom she merely despises. In Katz's re-
construction, much of Stein's time was spent
with relatives and girlfriends, sitting around
the house analyzing each other according
to strange systems of disapproval. A neurotic
young woman with a harelip named Annette
Rosenshine, who had been brought to Paris
from San Francisco by Stein's brother Michael
and his wife, Sarah (who had also settled in

Paris and were part of the analyzing group), became a special "patient" of Gertrude's and evidently almost expired from the daily sessions of, as Katz writes, "cryptic formulae, bludgeonings, denunciations and ephemeral suggestions for helping herself that bewildered the woman but that she had to accept on faith." Harriet Levy, also from San Francisco (she was Toklas's roommate in Paris for two years), was another victim of Stein's therapy. Stein seemed to dislike her even more than she disliked Rosenshine, and wrote about her with relentless malice. "Note in Harriet the absolute lack of self-restraint in eating in general dirtiness of habit of busting things," she says in one entry. In another (pairing Levy with an equally despicable Claribel Cone) she writes, "Harriet is sordid and brilliant and fairly mean. Claribel is big and inchoate and bland, both have an incredible amount of vanity which is probably the correlative of the passion for comfort.[5] They are not egoists really. they don't exist vitally enough to be that." And: "Harriet is a pill. she is a stinker."

Even Alice Toklas isn't spared Stein's hate-
fulness. "She is low clean through to the bottom crooked," Stein writes of her future life
partner, now just another person to trash, and
goes on: "a liar of the most sordid, unillumined,
undramatic unimaginative prostitute type,
coward, ungenerous, conscienceless, mean, vulgarly triumphant and remorseless, caddish, in
short just plain rotten low like Zobel but not
dangerous not effective, no evil. . . . Absolutely no distinguishing sense for people. Self-
knowledge but no consciousness of the significant, of the meaning of the things she knows,
the practical intelligence of the Hellenising
Jew but not the practical instinct as Stern has
it." And "Alice runs herself by her intellect but
there is not enough intellect in her to go around
and so she fails in every way."

One of the great coups of Katz's interview
with Toklas was his identification of May Bookstaver as the woman who broke Stein's heart.
Under Katz's velvet-gloved prodding, Toklas
confirmed that Bookstaver was the original of
the character Helen in *Q.E.D.*, and went on to

tell him that almost all of the book's dialogue was based on letters between Stein and Bookstaver, which, as Katz writes in a footnote, "Miss Stein had before her and followed closely during the writing of the book." Unfortunately, Katz continues, "The correspondence of dialogue and letters cannot be verified. When the novel came to light in 1932, and Miss Toklas discovered its biographical connection, she destroyed all Miss Bookstaver's letters 'in a passion.'" But this does not deter Katz—emboldened perhaps by Stein's confession in *The Making of Americans* that she cannot invent—from taking Toklas at her word and treating the dialogue of *Q.E.D.* as interchangeable with what passed in the post between Stein and Bookstaver. Katz argues that Stein's desperate thirst to understand everyone in the world derived in great part from the agony of her inability to fathom her lover. He sees the shadow of the affair hovering over *The Making of Americans* and giving it much of its intensity. Katz's dissertation goes on to examine other influences on Stein's typology (among them a book called *Sex and Character* by the brilliant and crazy anti-Semite Jew Otto Weininger), but his commentary on the Bookstaver romance is the work's white-hot center, the source of its fame and mana.

During my meetings with Ulla Dydo, Edward Burns, and William Rice, Katz had often come into the conversation, and emerged as a magnetic, larger-than-life figure. The trio always used the word "brilliant" about him and spoke of his interview with Toklas as a decisive event of Stein scholarship; it gleamed in their collective imagination as a kind of wondrous fable of charm and guile in the service of literature.

Dydo met Katz in 1955, when both were teaching at Vassar. "We immediately became good friends," she said. "We did a lot of talking. And he did a wonderful production of 'The Mother of Us All,' which I still remember. I remember it in my bones." Dydo went on to tell a story about Katz's dissertation which cleared up a minor mystery for me. In his prefatory acknowledgments, after citing Toklas and Gallup and various academic eminences, Katz writes, "Beyond all others is my debt to Mother Adele Fiske of Mahattanville, to whom it is impossible to express adequately my gratitude for ministrations on behalf of this labor. Her devotion and her generosity were overwhelming and humbling." I wondered what the nun had done to merit such gratitude. What had her ministrations been? Dydo related that Katz had had to leave Vassar because he had not finished his dissertation. "The rules are that if you don't finish your dissertation within three years you have to look elsewhere for a job. Leon then went to teach at Manhattanville College, and the mother superior there understood what was going on with that dissertation. He was not writing it. And she gave him orders. 'You will leave at my door every night a certain number of pages'—I don't know how many, it doesn't matter. And he did. A mother—a real mother—is no good for that. A girlfriend, a boyfriend, an anything

friend is no good for that. But a mother superior is excellent for that. I had tried—a bit. All
of us had tried one way or another. But she was
the one who got the Ph.D. out of him."

No Mother Adele appeared to get the annotated notebooks out of Katz. However, over the
years, he has dispensed to colleagues, like tid-
bits thrown to dogs, secrets Toklas told him that
he didn't include in the dissertation. Dydo and
Burns have been leading recipients of Katz's
largesse. In *Gertrude Stein: The Language That
Rises*, for example, Dydo writes: "According to
Leon Katz . . . the quarrel [between Stein and
Toklas] continued off and on until the second
visit to Chicago, in March 1935, when Stein told
Toklas she would leave her unless she stopped
goading and bickering. Toklas told Katz she
did stop." This stunning revelation appears
nowhere in the Stein biographical literature—
the very idea of Stein and Toklas splitting up
seems inconceivable—but such is Katz's authority as the winkler-out of Toklas's secrets,
that it simply didn't occur to Dydo to doubt its
truth, or to seek corroboration elsewhere.

Gertrude Stein and Alice B. Toklas arriving in Chicago,
November 7, 1934. Photograph by Carl Van Vechten.

Burns liked to tell the story of how Katz extracted the story of Bookstaver from Toklas by allowing her to believe he knew more than he did. "Leon had got wind of the affair from one of the people he interviewed, and when he uttered the name 'May Bookstaver' to Alice, she assumed that he knew everything. Actually he only knew one little detail." Dydo seamlessly continued Burns's story: "She said to him, 'Katz'—she always referred to him as 'Katz,' never as 'Leon'—'Katz, you're a detective,' and then she told him everything."

Another canonical story from the Katz/Toklas encounter has to do with Katz's handling of the delicate matter of Stein's malevolent descriptions of Toklas. "Leon waited until almost the end of his interviews with Alice before showing her the pages where Gertrude says horrible things about her," Burns said. "He had prepared her for it—he had told her how difficult this would be, how it might send her into God knows what state. She greeted him at the door with 'Give it to me,' and retired into the bedroom with the transcript. When she emerged she said, 'At least she didn't accuse me of disloyalty.'"

Toklas could not have taken pleasure in Stein's unpleasant portrait of herself, but she may not have been seriously afflicted by it, either. Many happily married couples—in life and in fiction—can't stand each other when they first meet. Stein's entries about Alice must have been written before they fell in love. That they did so had momentous consequences for Stein's art. Toklas liked and apparently understood *The Making of Americans* when no one else did. Leo had cruelly dismissed his sister's writing as incompetent. After Stein showed Toklas some pages of the book, and Toklas found the experience (as she recalls in her 1963 memoir *What Is Remembered*) "more exciting than anything else had ever been," she began typing the manuscript. The transformation of the dirty scraps of paper into clean pages of typescript was surely a pivotal event in the life of the work, which might well have foundered on Stein's anxiety about the maddening complexity of what she had undertaken. Toklas's belief in Stein's genius, made manifest by the growing pile of typed pages, emboldened Stein in her excruciating endeavor. She celebrates "the perfect joy of finding someone, any one really liking something you are liking, making, doing, being," in a memorable passage:

> It is a very strange feeling when one is loving a clock that is to every one of your class of living an ugly and a foolish one and one really likes such a thing and likes it very much and liking it is a serious thing, or one likes a colored handkerchief that is very gay and every one of your kind of living thinks it a very ugly or a foolish thing and thinks you like it because it is a funny thing to like it and you like it with a serious feeling, or you like eating something and liking it is a childish thing to every one or you like something that is a dirty thing and no one can really like that thing or you write a book and while you write it you are ashamed for every one must think you a silly or a crazy one and yet you write it and you are ashamed, you know you will be laughed at or pitied by every one and you have a queer feeling and you are not very certain and you go on writing. Then some one says yes to it, to something you are liking, or doing or making and then never again can you have completely such a feeling of being afraid and ashamed that you

had then when you were writing or liking the thing and not any one had said yes about the thing.

Someone says yes to it. The narrator's confusion and despair is to continue, but it is to be the confusion and despair of someone who knows she is "a great author inside one." As the "someone" who is validating Stein's work (and perhaps her lesbianism as well, as the images of odd clocks and colored handkerchiefs and "dirty things" seem to be obscurely signaling), Toklas is obviously no longer the low, brainless creature of the early notebook portrait. She is now the literary wife, the nurse who takes care of the writer-patient as he endures the illness of creation and its almost equally afflicting aftermath of publication. (In the case of Stein, the afflicting aftermath was usually nonpublication. *The Making of Americans,* for example, completed in 1911, was not published until 1925, in an edition of five hundred copies. Even then no happiness followed. In 1926, Stein received a mortifying letter from her publisher,

Robert McAlmon, reminding her that the book's publication was "a philanthropic enterprise" and threatening to pulp the many copies that hadn't sold.)

In *What Is Remembered* Toklas renders a mysterious passage between herself and Stein on the second day of their acquaintance. They had met the previous afternoon at the Michael Steins' and Toklas had been dazzled. "She was a golden brown presence, burned by the Tuscan sun and with a golden glint in her warm brown hair," Toklas writes, and goes on to speak of Stein's wonderful voice—"deep, full, velvety like a great contralto's, like two voices"—and of her "beautifully modeled and unique head," like a Roman emperor's. Stein invites Toklas to come to her house the next day, and then go for a walk, but when Toklas arrives at 27 rue de Fleurus a half hour late, Stein "had not her smiling countenance of the day before. She was now a vengeful goddess and I was afraid. I did not know what had happened or what was going to happen. Nor is it possible for me to tell about it now. After she had paced for some time about the long Florentine table . . . she stood in front of me and said, Now you understand. It is over. It is not too late to go for a walk. You can look at the pictures while I change my clothes."

Toklas's lateness does not account for Stein's fury (in fact, Toklas had sent Stein a *petit bleu* earlier in the day alerting her to her probable lateness). The passage is full of gaps. "I did not know what had happened or what was going to happen. Nor is it possible for me to tell about it now." To tell about what? Toklas is both telling and not telling. Her elusive sentences (written when she was in her eighties) gesture at secret meanings. The scene is like a dream. The little drama enacted in it is surely shorthand for some larger drama. We can only imagine what that drama was. But as the scene indicates—and the notebooks confirm—Stein and Toklas did not set out on their walk through life together quite as decisively and serenely as the legend has it. Much had to happen before Stein's dire view of Toklas gave way to the passionate love she expresses in her

erotic poetry (most famously—and endlessly—
in the poem "Lifting Belly").

Stein and Toklas lived together for nearly
forty years, and Stein's death left a shattered
Toklas. "Now she is gone and there can never
be happiness again," she wrote in August 1946
to Saxe Commins, an editor at Random House.
And, to Van Vechten, a month later, "Oh Carlo
could such perfection such happiness and such
beauty have been and here and now be gone
away." But her grief did not diminish—indeed
only strengthened—her literary wife's zeal. She
oversaw the publication by Yale of Stein's unpublished (some might still say unpublishable)
writings—eight volumes of them, with introductions by carefully chosen and in some cases
thoroughly baffled friends. And she fiercely
guarded Stein's reputation against all real or
imagined threats. "Gertrude's memory is all
my life," she wrote to Donald Gallup in March
1947. And (to Mercedes de Acosta in 1956) "If
there were not still things to do for Gertrude
there would be no reason for me to live on."
Part of her job, as she saw it, was to guard

Stein's life from prying eyes. Biographers were given evasive and, if necessary, untrue answers to questions. She herself "refused" to be written about. In September 1950, after an interview with John Malcolm Brinnin, one of Stein's early biographers, she proudly reported to Van Vechten, "I got him to exclude me from his book because the atmosphere of Baby's home was a private matter."

However, in 1955, when another biographer, an Englishwoman named Elizabeth Sprigge, threatened to give up her project after Toklas said, "I refuse to be mentioned," Toklas backed down. At the time, Sprigge seemed like a good thing for the Baby cause—she had written a well-received biography of August Strindberg—and Toklas didn't want to lose her. Later she did not think Sprigge was a good thing at all, referring to her as "La Sprigge" and pointing out "La Sprigge's unworthiness." When Sprigge's bland biography *Gertrude Stein: Her Life and Work,* came out two years later, Toklas had the satisfaction of seeing it savaged in the *New Republic* by her friend Gilbert Harrison, then the magazine's owner and editor.

Sprigge was a woman of her time, which may not have been the best time to be a woman. As she emerges from the journal she kept of her research (now at Yale), she is flirtatious, pleased with herself, and given to exclaiming over the beauty of Paris and writing down everything she ate ("a very chic sandwich with soft black bread and veal on the terrasse at Webers"). The journal records the rise and fall of her relations with Toklas, which begin with exchanges of delicate spring flowers and end in a muddle of mutual dislike. Unlike Katz, who patiently kept at his task of extracting classified information from the old woman, Sprigge cannot resist a contest of wills. She refuses the role of the quietly treacherous interviewer, preferring to remain the spunky heroine of her own drama, as in this exchange:

> When Alice opened the door to me I thanked her.
> A. What for? said Alice. For opening the door?
> E. Yes.
> A. Nobody ever thanks one for opening the door.

E. Don't they?

A. Not in America nor in France.

E. Well, I do. Do you mind?

A. It's rather a shock.

E. Then I'm afraid it will have to be.

A. What's the matter. You seem to have got out of bed the wrong side.

E. On the contrary. I have just had an extremely gay luncheon on the street corner with Basil Rakoczi.

Near the end of her journal, Sprigge records a conversation with Thornton Wilder at the Continental Hotel in Paris, who asks, "Has Alice a scunner against you?" and, when she tells him about "the gradual cooling of Alice's feelings for me," he says, "You are up against a lot of things. First those girls, *ces dames la,* never really like or trust women. They like men as an audience, preferably young men, but anything in pants they prefer to a woman. There's a young man called Katz. . . . She'll give him far more than she's given you though she'll tell him not to publish it." Sprigge had met Katz the previous winter in New York—"we talked for four hours and went out to lunch—and we are friends"—but had no inkling of what Toklas had already "given" him. She renders him as "a Russian Jew in the early thirties. . . . Very serious, gentle, melancholy and adores Alice."

During the first year of my acquaintance with Burns, Dydo, and Rice they urged me to do two things—to read *The Making of Americans* and to interview Leon Katz. For a long time, I resisted their urgings. Then, in the winter of 2004, when I was preparing for a trip to California (where Katz then lived), I gave in to the notion that Katz was a necessary stop on any journey into the Stein interior, and telephoned him. He warily consented to meet me, making many conditions, among them that he would not talk about his interview with Toklas because he would be writing about it in his own book, and didn't want to be "scooped." I agreed to his terms, and plans were made for meeting at a Los Angeles airport near his house. "Leon is a real person," Dydo had said. "He's the kind of person you would find interesting, if I may say so, and I think I have the sense of what interests you, a little bit. You can say, 'Will it be a pleasure?' I don't know. It will certainly be of interest and what's of interest is a pleasure." On the telephone, Katz was as Dydo had described him. His realness and real charm came through and I looked forward to the meeting—which, however, never took place. A mix-up about the date—he came to the airport on February 4 and I had plane tickets for the next day—put an end to all possibility of interviewing Katz. He had been ambivalent from the start, and now the balance tipped in the direction of flight. He graciously accepted blame for the mix-up, but declined to meet on the fifth—or on any other day.

When I reported the non-interview to Dydo, Burns, and Rice, their response was an unexpected release of suppressed anger. They took the mix-up to be Katz's fault, a typical evasive action, and a kind of last straw. I myself was not so sure that the mix-up was Katz's fault. I had my own ambivalence to consider; his conditions had irked me. But even after I persuaded the scholars to suspend judgment on the question of whose unconscious had misbehaved, they continued venting their resentment against Katz for his failure to produce the annotated edition of the notebooks. They felt frustrated and in some fundamental sense betrayed.

"This man has been sitting on this material for fifty years," Burns said. "No one has seen it. The book needs to be done. I once offered to take a sabbatical and work with him on it. But he ignored the offer. There is something deep inside himself that is preventing him from writing it."

"There was always a reason," Dydo said. "He had to make money, he had to support his aging parents. If it wasn't the aging parents, it was something else. He had very good jobs. He taught in the theater departments at the University of Pittsburgh, Carnegie Mellon, Cornell, Yale, and UCLA. He also wrote avant-garde plays, good ones. Eddie and I had many exchanges with him in the early years, we had many questions about Gertrude and Alice. We would call him and he would answer. Then gradually over the years there was less and less of that."

"In the early years we would ask him how the work on the book was coming," Burns said. "Then we ceased asking."

"What does he look like?" I said, caught in the spell of the absent and yet always present Katz.

"He's good-looking," Dydo said.

"Now completely white hair," Burns said.

"He takes good care of his body," Dydo said.

"Is he small or large?" I asked. Sprigge's "Russian Jew" had evoked a bearded man of slight build.

"He's tall and broad," Dydo said.

"But stooped a little by age now," Burns said. "The thing I always remember about Leon is the ring. A huge ring."

"He always lived in beautiful apartments," Dydo said. "Spacious, well-appointed, good lay-outs, expensive."

Burns expressed his outrage over the e-mail Katz had sent me to sever our relations. Katz had written:

To avoid the slightest misunderstanding, I must repeat once more what I spelled out on the phone during our first conversation, and add a word as well. . . . I am scrupulous in my determination not to have my material used by anyone before my own book . . . is out. It constitutes a labor of many years and much thought, and I am very much determined that its originality, both in facts still generally unknown concerning those early years, and in my own cogitations about them, are not made use of piecemeal in other authors' works, leaving my own to be regarded as revisiting already known material.

Katz went on to insist that I not quote from or draw on his dissertation. "That letter must have come as a shock to you," Burns said. "Like the closing of a gate. 'You may not write about me. You may not use my work.' 'What do you mean? What you've done is out there. It's published.'"

As it happened, Katz's letter had not shocked me. I understood and empathized with his concerns. I knew very well why he didn't want to discuss the Toklas interview: he was afraid I would steal his narrative. His strictures about his dissertation were preposterous, yes—a dissertation is a published text and may be summarized, drawn on, and quoted—but his fear of being ripped off was not irrational. Narrative theft is a common phenomenon. An example of it had been held up by Burns himself a few weeks earlier. To his dismay, a recent writer on Stein had appropriated a charming narrative he had created out of laborious archival research and published as an appendix in one of his collections of letters. The writer had acknowledged Burns as a source of information for the story, but not as its author.

Although, strictly speaking, narrative theft is a form of plagiarism, it is such a subtle form that it is rarely if ever prosecuted. A writer who reprints another writer's sentences and paragraphs without quotation marks is clearly breaking the law, but a writer who filches another writer's arrangement of facts is much less clearly crossing a line. The author Burns was upset about did nothing that thousands of nonfiction writers haven't done. She might have more clearly acknowledged her debt to Burns, but she didn't have to, and she may not even have been aware of the degree of her indebtedness. Good stories have a quality of authorlessness. The better they are, the more authorless they seem. They give the sense of being out there, like facts. Burns is hardly the first writer to experience the indignity—and compliment—of narrative theft. I have experienced it myself; and for this reason I did not take the umbrage at Katz's letter that Dydo, Burns, and Rice did on my behalf, but felt I knew exactly what he was talking about. Even if he never writes his book, he is entitled not to make a present of its plot to a stranger, and he is right to fear what a stranger may obliviously make off with from his published writings.

"So what is the answer about Katz? Or what is the question?" I asked, paraphrasing a famous line of Stein's, the words she was supposed to have uttered on her deathbed. On

July 27, 1946, Stein was operated on, at the
American Hospital in Paris, for what proved to
be inoperable stomach cancer and died before
coming out of anesthesia. In *What Is Remembered*, Toklas wrote of the "troubled, confused
and very uncertain" afternoon of the surgery.
"I sat next to her and she said to me early in
the afternoon, What is the answer? I was silent.
In that case, she said, what is the question?"
However, in a letter to Van Vechten written ten
years earlier, Toklas had written: "About Baby's
last words. She said upon waking from a sleep—
What is the question. And I didn't answer
thinking she was not completely awakened.
Then she said again—What is the question
and before I could speak she went on—If there
is no question then there is no answer."

Stein's biographers have naturally selected
the superior "in that case what is the question?" version. Strong narratives win out over
weak ones when no obstacle of factuality stands
in their way. What Stein actually said remains
unknown. That Toklas cited the lesser version in a letter of 1953 is suggestive, but not
conclusive.

"My question is," I said to Dydo, Burns, and Rice, "Why are you so mad at Katz? Why does it matter to you that he hasn't published the annotated notebooks?"

The answer came out slowly and hesitantly and was intertwined with *The Making of Americans* itself. The three scholars place Katz's un-written book and Stein's unread masterpiece in a kind of tragic clasp. They believe that had Katz fulfilled his early promise as the pre-eminent authority on *The Making of Americans,* Stein's novel could well be on college reading lists today. They feel that the surge of criticism necessary to propel a work into the academic canon would have followed upon the publication of the annotated notebooks. As it is, *The Making of Americans* remains an academic pariah, unstudied, unassigned, unread. Not all of this neglect can be laid at the feet of Katz, of course. The work itself, the scholars are aware, is innately rebarbative. And, unlike *Ulysses* and *The Waste Land* and other monuments of literary modernism, it offers few if any of the literary allusions to which academic criticism is drawn. For that reason,

Katz's biographical findings glint with special significance.

"Leon was charged to write the book that would have created a path toward the novel," Burns said. "His interview with Alice was a last living link to its composition."

"He's left us hanging," Dydo said. "And we'd like to hit him over the head and open that head up and see what's in it—assuming there's something in it. We're not entirely sure anymore."

At the end of the meeting, Burns handed me a videotape he had once spoken of, but had hitherto been unable to find. I played it that night, and there was Alice Toklas (impersonated by an actress who vaguely resembled her), lying in bed and soliloquizing about the "young man with the innocent face" who had come to interview her years before and in whom she had confided lurid secrets about her life with Gertrude Stein. The Alice impersonator lies back on her cushions, her fingers

plucking at a white crocheted shawl, and recalls how "that very inquisitive young man"
sat with her hour after hour as "the cold and
the dark and the wet of Paris winter" crept
into her apartment and "I told him all of that";
namely, about sex with Gertrude—"The smell
and the taste of Baby. . . . The filth we talked.
Sweet, sweet flesh"—and about her jealous
rage over the May Bookstaver affair. She recalls the satisfaction she took in her indiscretions. "Telling that boy, his pencil scribbling.
It was detestable telling him such things. For
him or for me? Not for me. Because I knew
exactly what I was doing. The pleasure of looking into that stranger's face and betraying Gertrude as she had betrayed me." Alice goes on,
"I told him how I destroyed our life together
for a year and more than a year. . . . I told him
how I screamed, 'Damn you, Gertrude, damn
you.'"

The author of the monologue is Leon Katz,
who else. The Toklas piece, along with two
other of Katz's monologues, was performed in
Los Angeles in 2000, and filmed the same year.

It offers few, if any, surprises to the Stein scholar. The secrets Toklas theatrically utters from her bed are the same ones Katz more calmly retails in his dissertation. But here and there Katz takes liberties that put into question the factuality of the monologue—and perhaps even of the dissertation itself. In the monologue, Toklas babbles about standing over Stein and forcing her to change "may" to "can." As we know, this scene comes out of Ulla Dydo's tour de force of imaginative scholarship, built on Katz's footnote about the "passion" by which Toklas was seized when she found out about May Bookstaver. The real Toklas never confessed her savaging of *Stanzas in Meditation* to Katz or to anyone else.

No one has ever seen Katz's notes of his interview with Toklas. We have only his word that Toklas told him what he says she did. With one exception, there is no corroborating evidence of any of his citations of or quotations from the interview. The exception, paradoxically, is Dydo's discovery of the "may"/"can" business. If Katz's anachronistic inclusion of it in his monologue raises questions about his dissertation, the discovery itself puts them to rest: the documentary evidence of Toklas's rage corroborates Katz's account of what the rage was about.

In a final chapter of the dissertation, Katz wonderfully expresses his sense of the importance for Stein of writing *The Making of Americans*. "After the novel was finished, the portentous subject, the effort to achieve the grand manner, even the terms of formal intellectual discourse are all discarded, and her writing settles into a life-long, smiling, personal pageantry of the nearby and the trivial," he writes. "Germinating out of nine years of labor on a novel that passed beyond the scope and limits of the novel's form, from the settled center of her matured vision, out of the 'flattening' of the hierarchies of thought and feeling that her intensity of vision finally achieved, her unique art subsequently emerged as an endlessly full hymn of pleasure in the actual, a nonselective tribute to the uniform splendors of existence." Katz himself, after his years of intense engagement with the forces by which Stein's anti-novel was shaped, may, too, have felt the sense of a feat pulled off and the urge to move on. Dydo, Burns, and Rice's regret over Katz's defection from the world of Stein scholarship may be nothing compared with Katz's relief in being free of its difficulties and uncertainties.

PART THREE

In *Wars I Have Seen,* Gertrude Stein writes of the remarkable kindness of a young Frenchman named Paul Genin, the owner of a silk factory in Lyon and a country neighbor, who came to her after America entered World War II and asked if she needed money. She did—the funds from America on which she and Toklas depended no longer arrived— and he offered her a matching monthly stipend. Stein and Toklas lived on Genin's kindness for six months, after which Stein sold a Cézanne ("quite quietly to some one who came to see me") and no longer needed money. "And so I thanked Paul Genin and paid him back and he said if you ever need me just tell me, and that was that."

Stein goes on to reflect, "Life is funny that way. It always is funny that way, the ones that naturally should offer do not, and those who have no reason to offer it, do, you never know you never do know where your good fortune is to come from."

There is another story illustrating life's funniness that Stein might have told in *Wars I Have Seen*. A few weeks after the first chapter of this book appeared in the *New Yorker,* an accusatory letter appeared in the magazine's letters column. The letter cited the infamous Gestapo raid of an orphanage in the village of Izieu from which forty-four Jewish children between the ages of four and seventeen and their seven supervisors were seized and ultimately shipped to death camps. The orphanage, the correspondent wrote, was "not far from Stein and Toklas's house in Culoz" and, "in the light of this history, Stein's comment in *Wars I Have Seen* about becoming frightened only after the American soldiers arrived and she began 'hearing what had happened to others' is somewhat hard to believe." I spoke to Ulla Dydo and Ed Burns and Bill Rice about the troubling question this letter raised, and they suggested that I write to someone in Paris who might actually be able to answer it. This was Paul Genin's stepdaughter, Joan Chapman, who had been in close touch with Stein and Toklas at the time of the Izieu raid and would be apt to know what they knew or didn't know. I wrote to Joan Chapman and received this reply:

> No, we had no idea that a group of Jewish children were hidden in a boarding school at Izieu, they were indeed deported, we only found out months later. I'm sure Gertrude and Alice had no idea of the incident at the time. Izieu is about 20 K from Belley and 30 K from Culoz. In those days the only way of getting to and fro was walking or on a bike, people were pretty isolated from each other. Anything confidential was never mentioned by phone.

Joan Chapman went on to tell this story:

> One day about that time my mother was asked by someone who ran an orphanage for

Alice B. Toklas and Gertrude Stein with Basket II
at Culoz, in the 1940s.

Spanish Republican children refugees, to hide the only Jewish child in her care. His name was Manfred Iudas, he was 5 years old, he was German, he only spoke Spanish! As a matter of course Gertrude came over to make his acquaintance, he was a charming, beautiful child. After a month or so my mother had grown very fond of him and she decided to adopt him. Gertrude was consulted and she said no you can't do that, he must be adopted by a Jewish family, I cannot remember quite how that was managed but it was.

The story chills the blood and more than confirms the view that Stein did not behave well in World War II. To propose that a Jewish child be sent to a Jewish family at a time when everywhere in France Jews were being rounded up was an act of almost inconceivable callousness. Dydo and Burns and Rice agreed that Stein's advice was inexplicable and terrible. We imagined together the tragic fate of the beautiful little boy.

A year later, when Joan Chapman was visiting America, I met with her and questioned her about the incident of the Jewish child.

As we talked—as more details about the incident emerged—the story changed. As its bare bones took on flesh, Stein's interference no longer damned her. The writer of the accusatory letter had dated the Izieu raid April 6, 1943, but in fact it took place on April 6, 1944, four months before France was liberated. Joan Chapman assured me that Stein's advice had not put Manfred Iudas's life at risk; the child went to the Jewish family only after Liberation. There had never been a question of his leaving the Genin household until all danger for Jews had passed. Joan Chapman had not realized that her laconic account could be read as a condemnation of Stein. She assumed that we knew what she knew.

The instability of human knowledge is one of our few certainties. Almost everything we know we know incompletely at best. And almost nothing we are told remains the same when retold. When Joan Chapman, who is an attractive and vigorous woman of eighty, with an excellent memory, retold the story of Manfred Iudas, she said that a second child had come with him from the orphanage, an older, non-Jewish boy. She did not remember why this boy came—perhaps to keep Manfred company? She couldn't say. The second boy exemplified the fat we cut off when we compose a lean narrative. Under my questioning, Joan Chapman told the story of the Jewish boy as a story of regret for herself and her mother, Nena.

"He was adorable," she said of the child. "He was very bright. And he looked uncannily like a nephew of my mother's. My mother and Paul couldn't have children. He would have been a wonderful boy for them to have. And I would have been very pleased to have a brother. I regretted him. I regretted him for a long time."

Joan Chapman told me how her family became acquainted with Stein and Toklas. Her mother, leafing through the local telephone directory, was astonished to see the name Gertrude Stein. She called Stein's number and Stein answered the phone. "Are you Gertrude Stein?" Nena asked. "Yes." "Are you *the* Gertrude Stein?" "Yes." Nena told Stein that

she had just moved into the neighborhood
and Stein said, "I'll be right over." Stein barely
mentions Nena and Joan in *Wars I Have Seen*.
We know from *The Autobiography of Alice B.
Toklas* that Stein's interest in young men (Paul
Genin was in his mid-thirties at the time of his
loan) did not extend to their wives. At her
gatherings in the rue de Fleurus she assigned
Alice to sit with them. "Before I decided to
write this book, my twenty-five years with
Gertrude Stein, I had often said that I would
write the wives of geniuses I have sat with.
I have sat with so many," Stein mischievously
wrote. However, in the case of the Genins,
Stein did not favor Paul over his wife. Joan
Chapman remembers being jealous of Stein's
attention to her mother: "She liked me, but
she liked my mother more. Gertrude was like
the sun—very warm. I adored her. She had a
beautiful face. She had beautiful brown eyes,
she had lovely hands. She was much better
looking than Alice, who was hideous. Alice was
all sort of spiky. She looked like a witch. She
had this mustache. Alice was not warm and

welcoming, not as nice as Gertrude. I remember feeling that Alice had another look on us. She didn't need people the way Gertrude did. Gertrude needed to see us because it fed her art. She never invented anything, apparently. We saw her three or four times a week when they lived in Bilignin. When they moved to Culoz, it was once a week. After the war we hardly saw them. Gertrude was lionized by all those people."

"She dropped you?"

"Yes. You must understand, she was suddenly in the midst of all those people arriving and making a fuss over her. . . . Those wonderful people. We weren't very interesting, were we?"

"Did you mind?"

"Oh, yes. I think my mother did very much. But Paul now says, 'Well, *c'est normal.* Gertrude saw us because she was bored—she had to see somebody.'" Paul is ninety-seven and still owns property near Bilignin.

Joan Chapman returned to the subject of the Jewish boy. "My mother talked to Gertrude about it and Gertrude said, 'No way. He's a

Jewish child and has to be adopted by Jewish parents.' It was an extraordinary thing to say because Gertrude was not a practicing Jew."

But in fact, given that the child's safety was not at stake, it was not such an extraordinary thing for Stein—or for any Jew (practicing or nonpracticing)—to say. As one of Isaac Bashevis Singer's characters puts it, "The whole point of Jewishness is isolation." Stein kept her Jewishness out of her work and out of her public persona, but she never abjured it. When she was twenty-two she wrote a paper for a Radcliffe writing class in "argumentative composition" entitled "The Modern Jew Who Has Given Up the Faith of His Fathers Can Reasonably and Consistently Believe in Isolation." "Isolation means no intermarriage with an alien," the young Stein wrote, and went on, "The Jew shall marry only the Jew. He may have business friends among the Gentiles, he may mix with them in their work and in their pleasures, he will go to their schools and receive their instructions, but in the sacred precincts of the home, in the close union of family and kinsfolk he must be a Jew with Jews; the Gentile has no place there." Fifty years later, she had evidently not changed her views; her horror at the idea of a Jewish boy living out his childhood in a Gentile home is of a piece with them.

At the end of the paper, Stein writes, "So long as the Jews keep themselves isolated so long are they bound to be subject to persecution to a greater or less extent. We must ask whether they gain enough by this exclusion to make it worth while to be in this attitude of separateness and persecution. Yes I think they do!" The compensation, she writes, is the unbreakable bond between Jews everywhere: "Ask any Israelite no matter how liberal, no matter how numerous and intimate are his Christian friends; ask him to tell you to whom he would rather appeal if he were in any need either spiritual or material, whether he would rather go to a perfect stranger a Jew or to his most intimate Christian friend and without hesitation he will reply, 'To the Jew every time.'"

On this point, the young and the mature

Stein do not agree. The mature Stein would go
to the Christian every time. Pablo Picasso, Juan
Gris, Carl Van Vechten, Thornton Wilder, Ernest
Hemingway, Bernard Faÿ, W. G. Rogers, Fran-
cis Rose—her great friends (and ultimately, in
some cases, great enemies) were goyim. We
know of no Jew to whom Stein turned in spiritual or material need. To be sure, her "marriage" was to a Jew, and she remained close to
the family of her oldest brother, Michael. But
the world she describes in *The Autobiography of
Alice B. Toklas* is as far from the world of Isaac
Singer as one can come. As she grew into her
role of modernist genius, the "Jewish question" seems to have faded from her consciousness; the vehemence of her reaction to Nena's
wish to adopt Manfred Iudas was a piece of
momentary atavism.

But what do we know? Perhaps Stein had a
secret Jewish life. Biography and autobiography are the aggregate of what, in the former,
the author happens to learn, and, in the latter,
he chooses to tell. A cache of letters between
Stein and a rabbi may be discovered that will
cast a whole new light on Stein's Jewish iden-

tity. Such discoveries are a regular inconvenience of the biographical enterprise.

A rabbi, as it happens, has unexpectedly turned up in Alice Toklas's biography. He is casually mentioned in a 1997 memoir by the Polish-born opera singer Doda Conrad, who lived and worked in Paris, and befriended Toklas in the last period of her life. Conrad writes of his chance encounter with Toklas in the early nineteen-fifties:

> Waiting in line in front of a cinema on the Avenue de l'Opéra to attend the presentation of Marc Allégret's film about André Gide (to which I had been invited), I found myself standing behind an odd little woman. I recognized Alice B. Toklas by her inimitable floppy hat with ostrich feathers, her stunning yellow sandals, her gendarme-like whiskers, and all the rest. She looked lost, with her invitation, and seemed not to know which ticket booth to go to. I offered to help her but did not reveal that I had recognized her in order not to upset her.

Alice B. Toklas in 1949.
Photograph by Carl Van Vechten.

After the film, as Conrad helps her find a taxi, Toklas introduces herself and says, "Your name must be Doda, because you look surprisingly like the singer Doda Conrad." He goes on, "Flattered that she had recognized me, I was even more enchanted to have met her." A week later, Conrad comes to tea at Toklas's elegant apartment at 5 rue Christine. He rhapsodizes over the modernist masterpieces that entirely fill the walls of the salon, the luxe silver tea service, the dainty sandwiches and pâtisseries, the "atmosphere of exquisite hospitality." Then he writes,

> We immediately became friends, and she took me into her confidence, as if Alice had discovered in me someone with whom she could speak as an equal, which it appeared she had been unable to do for a long time. She told me about her trips to Poland, when she was a child, to visit her paternal grandfather. This grandfather was the rabbi of Ostrow, a small city near Kalisz, the cradle of the Tykociner, who were my ancestors. The rabbi's son had emigrated to San Francisco in the middle of the last century, where he had married a small

Spanish Jewess, a great beauty. Alice described the elegance of the excursions the rabbi organized for her when she was a child.

When Toklas wrote *What Is Remembered,* she had evidently forgotten the rabbi of Ostrow. She writes of a trip to Poland to visit her paternal grandparents but fails to identify the grandfather as a rabbi. The words "rabbi" and "Jew" are entirely absent from the autobiography. Toklas's un-Jewishness is one of her signatures. When a young Californian named Roland Duncan interviewed her in 1952 and cautiously approached the subject of Stein's Jewishness, he was smartly slapped on the wrist:

Duncan: Do you think possibly that [Stein] felt that there was any cultural or religious minority which would have set her apart—
Toklas: No.
Duncan: —perhaps made her strive toward certain social or cultural objectives? None at all?
Toklas: Never. We never had any feeling of any minority. We weren't the minority. We represented America.

When Toklas became a Catholic, in 1957, she went so far as to characterize the conversion not as a repudiation of Judaism but as a return to the Church. She told the writer Janet Flanner, in all seriousness, that she had been baptized in childhood when a Catholic friend of her parents sprinkled her with holy water. Flanner was also privy to Toklas's remarkable idea that she would be reunited in Heaven with Stein, who, as a genius, had been spared the fate of her fellow plain-dead Jews and was waiting for her there. (The non-genius Toklas had to make do with the mechanisms for eternal life open to ordinary observant Catholics.) Doda Conrad, Virgil Thomson, Donald Sutherland, and other friends of Toklas's old age have also reported this rigmarole.

Toklas's acknowledgment of her Jewish roots to Doda Conrad may be an example of the bonding that Stein celebrated in her paper on Jewish isolation. To a Jewish stranger, Toklas could say what she wouldn't say to her Christian friends—and to the readers of her autobiography, whom she imagined as goyim.

Linda Simon, in her *Biography of Alice B. Toklas*, establishes, through archival research, that Toklas's father, Ferdinand, married a woman from a German Jewish family named Emma Levinsky. So where does that leave the small Spanish Jewess? And whose invention is she? Ulla Dydo and Edward Burns and Bill Rice often spoke of Toklas as a liar. When I asked them to give me examples of her lies, they were at a loss, but adhered to their conviction of her untruthfulness. Doda Conrad's veracity is unknown to me. There is no doubt, however, that he and Janet Flanner were the chief support of Toklas in the sad final years of her life. Conrad wrote to Burns in 1971 of "the strange, inexplicable Alice B. Toklas episode, a fleeting moment in my life." He went on, "What induced me to 'take over,' as I did, after she broke her hipbone, early in 1964, was mainly the fact that nobody really made a move to do something. All her old friends (except Janet Flanner) were delighted and relieved to have the outsider Doda Conrad step in for them. (They sent checks, of course.)"

"I marvel at the extent to which I got in-

volved," Conrad wrote. "I truly took fait et cause for someone I did not really know and, probably, did not really like."

Confessions of not really liking Alice are a leitmotiv of the Stein/Toklas memoir literature. Stein always came first—and remained first—in the affections of those who knew the couple. In *When This You See Remember Me,* W. G. Rogers described Toklas thus: "The Miss Toklas I first saw in 1917 and last saw in 1947, was and has remained, a little stooped, somewhat retiring and self effacing. She doesn't sit in a chair, she hides in it; she doesn't look at you, but up at you; she is always standing just half a step outside the circle. She gives the appearance, in short, not of a drudge, but of a poor relation, someone invited to the wedding but not to the wedding feast." Privately, Rogers almost spelled out what he didn't say in print. Writing to Edward Burns in 1971, Rogers said, "Gertrude was our first and dearest friend in that household. We loved her very much and, I think, it can be said she loved us.

Alice came second, but a close second. Creatively I think Alice was not a close second but she was a unique person, less subtle than Gertrude, less sensitive, more obvious, but of a sharper register. . . . We loved Alice but we had our disagreements."

Rogers's association of Toklas with the figure of the poor relation proved to be a piece of prescience as well as a nice trope. In her last years Toklas sank into poverty; what Doda Conrad "took over" with Janet Flanner was the horrible tangle of Toklas's finances and the task of soliciting money from her friends to keep her (barely) afloat. Toklas's financial difficulties derived from Gertrude Stein's will. Stein did and didn't provide for her "wife" of forty years.

Stein wrote her will on July 23, 1947, after she had been diagnosed with stomach cancer and was awaiting the useless surgery that ended her existence. She left her money and her collection of paintings to Toklas—but only for "her use for life"—a momentary stop on the way to their true destination: Stein's nephew Allan, the only son of Michael Stein. Was this devotion to kin an object of Stein's never quite extinguished Jewishness? Or was it a mere expression of the deeply ingrained belief, shared by Christian and Jew alike, that money has to stay in the family? In *The House of the Seven Gables* Nathaniel Hawthorne wonderfully describes this conviction:

> But there is no one thing which men so rarely do, whatever the provocation or inducement, as to bequeath patrimonial property away from their own blood. They may love other individuals far better than their relatives; they may even cherish dislike, or positive hatred, to the latter; but yet, in view of death, the strong prejudice of propinquity revives, and impels the testator to send down his estate in the line marked out by custom, so immemorial, that it looks like nature.

Stein disliked Allan but still felt impelled to make him her heir. As it turned out, he died before Toklas did, and next in line were his three children, Daniel, from his first marriage, and Michael and Gabrielle, from his second. The first wife, Yvonne, plays no role in Toklas's biography; the second, Roubina (Toklas called her the Armenian), plays a large one. Stein's collection of modernist paintings—acquired for not much money in the first decade of the twentieth century—had become valuable. In her will Stein wrote that "insofar as it may become necessary for [Toklas's] proper maintenance and support, I authorize my Executors to make payments to her from the principal of my Estate, and, for that purpose, to reduce to cash any paintings or other personal property belonging to my Estate." This would seem to take care of Toklas very nicely. But it didn't.

Wills are uncanny and electric documents. They lie dormant for years, and then spring to life when their author dies, as if death were rain. Their effect on those they enrich or disappoint is never negligible, and sometimes unexpectedly charged. They thrust living and dead into a final fierce clasp of love or hatred. But they are not written in stone—for all their granite legal language—and they can be bent to subvert the wishes of the writer. Such was the case with Stein's will. The painting collection did not maintain and support Toklas in her fragile old age; in fact, in April 1961, while she was away at a spa in Italy taking a mud cure for arthritis, it was seized from her apartment. The Armenian, claiming that the paintings were not safe during Toklas's absence, had received legal authority to remove them to a vault in the Chase Manhattan Bank in Paris; when Toklas returned to the apartment, she found only their outlines on the walls.

In two pieces in the *New Yorker*—one in 1961 and the other in 1975—Janet Flanner traced a line leading from Stein's will to Roubina's brutal act. According to Flanner, much of Toklas's trouble stemmed from Stein's decision "on sound tax counsel" to place her estate under the jurisdiction of the probate court in Baltimore, and to the court's appointment of a man named Edgar Allan Poe (the poet's great-nephew) to administer it. (Stein named Toklas and Allan Stein executors, but for reasons no longer known they renounced or were forced to renounce this role, and Poe took it over.)

"Gertrude had been precise about how her funds were to be spent, but, unaccountably, Poe proved to be an obstructionist and parsi-

monious in fulfilling her wishes, of which he
seemed to disapprove, although it was none of
his business," Flanner wrote in her piece of
December 1975. As well as providing for Toklas, Stein had provided for her own literary immortality: "I desire my Executors hereinafter
named to pay to Carl Van Vechten, of 101 Cen-
tral Park, W., New York City, such sum of
money as the said Carl Van Vechten shall, in
his own absolute discretion, deem necessary
for the publication of my unpublished manuscripts." Flanner suggests that it was Poe's
dilatoriness both in funding the publication
of Stein's unpublished work and in sending
Toklas her monthly personal allowance of four
hundred dollars that drove her to the rash act
that precipitated the seizure of the paintings.
"Alice cajoled and threatened," Flanner writes.
"Poe sent money in driblets, and in 1954 Alice,
who was desperate, finally sold about forty
Picasso drawings without informing Poe." When
Roubina—who was "keeping a beady eye upon
the pictures in the interests of her minor
children"—discovered that the drawings were
gone, she began the legal proceedings that

ended in the raid on the apartment. In a letter of 1965, Daniel Stein (for all that he would be a beneficiary of his stepmother's interventions) wrote of Roubina with exuberant malice: she "has always been a devious, hypocritical, and thoroughly unprincipled being willing to stop at nothing to achieve her ends, whatever they were. She is something between a Mexican bandit and one of those Egyptian infiltrators who used to cross over into Israel and murder the children of the kibbutzim in their beds."

The minor characters of biography, like their counterparts in fiction, are less tenderly treated than major characters. The writer uses them to advance his narrative and carelessly drops them when they have performed their function. Look at how I have used poor Roubina! Unlike the flat characters of fiction (as E. M. Forster called them), who have no existence outside the novel they were invented to animate, the flat characters of biography are actual, three-dimensional people. But the biographer is writing a life not lives, and to keep

himself on course, must cultivate a kind of nar-
cissism on behalf of his subject that blinds him
to the full humanity of anyone else. As he turns
the bracing storylessness of human life into the
flaccid narrativity of biography, he cannot
worry about the people who never asked to be
dragged into his shaky enterprise.

One of the notable features of *The Autobiography of Alice B. Toklas* is Stein's high-handed
treatment of the lesser people in her circle. She
flattens them as perhaps no biographer has ever
flattened a character before or since. Stein was
both happy about and a little ashamed of the
success of this most artful of "audience" works.
By writing in Toklas's voice, Stein made herself
speak a more conventional English than the
English she speaks in the hermetic works, but
what the audience liked about the work wasn't
merely that it could understand it. The audience recognized that it had been given something truly original—the work is as advanced
and experimental, as wild and subversive as the
most advanced and experimental and wild and
subversive of Stein's works. It is—among the

other things it is—an anti-biography. Stein's presentation of herself in the book as one of the world's greatest geniuses, and of every other person as someone put on earth only to amuse or irritate her, is surely a reflection not of the way she saw herself and her friends but of the way she thought about biographical representation. Early in the book she writes of a servant named Hélène who worked for Stein and Leo in the early days of the rue de Fleurus salon:

> Hélène stayed with the household until the end of 1913. Then her husband, by that time she had married and had a little boy, insisted that she work for others no longer. To her great regret she left and later she always said that life at home was never as amusing as it had been at the rue de Fleurus. Much later, only about three years ago, she came back for a year, she and her husband had fallen on bad times and her boy had died. She was as cheery as ever and enormously interested. She said isn't it extraordinary, all those people whom I knew when they were nobody are now always mentioned in the newspapers, and the other

night over the radio they mentioned the name
of Monsieur Picasso.

Stein's heartlessness ("and her boy had died")
is like the heartlessness of Hilaire Belloc's *Cautionary Tales for Children*. The author of *Three
Lives* isn't really indifferent to the agony of a
mother who has lost her son. But she is not
writing *Three Lives;* she is writing a book
about how amusing life around Gertrude Stein
is. The heartlessness is essential to the amusement the reader feels as he is propelled along
the stream of Stein's grotesque gaiety and egotism. Every day brings satisfaction. And every
character is a foil for Stein's ultra-importance.
No one escapes diminishment. Even fellow geniuses like Picasso do not quite reach the pinnacle where Stein placidly sits, but hover a
little below it. "Now listen! I'm no fool," Stein
once said in reply to a student's question about
her line "Rose is a rose is a rose is a rose." "I
know that in daily life we don't go around saying 'is a . . . is a . . . is a . . .' Yes, I'm no fool; but
I think that in that line the rose is red for
the first time in English poetry for a hundred

years." Yet Stein's boastfulness never got in the way of her understanding of human insignificance. As a child, she had looked at the night sky and recoiled from astronomy's insult. "It was frightening when the first comet I saw made it real that the stars were worlds and the earth only one of them," she wrote in *Everybody's Autobiography*. "Dead is dead," she wrote in *The Making of Americans*. *The Autobiography of Alice B. Toklas* slyly mocks the immortality biography seeks to bestow on its subjects. If you listen to the book's music, you will catch the low hum of melancholy. If you regard it as an exercise in whistling in the dark, you will understand its brilliance.

After Stein's death, Toklas pursued the protection and perpetuation of Stein's legend with matchless zeal and devotion. At the same time, and without any slackening of her literary widow's efforts, Toklas came into her own as a personality. She no longer sat with the wives of geniuses. She began to have young men—if not young geniuses—of

her own. One of these, the novelist Donald
Windham, who had become acquainted with
Toklas in Rome in the spring of 1961, noted,
in a memoir called *The Roman Spring of
Alice B. Toklas*, that "graciousness—unapolo-
getic graciousness—was Alice Toklas's most
pervasive characteristic that spring: a graciousness that made her plain features appear
beautiful as soon as you were at ease with her."
Windham's memoir includes letters from Toklas to himself and his partner, Sandy Campbell, that illustrate the observation. Graciousness radiates from her letters to Windham and
Campbell and, indeed, from all her post-Stein
correspondence. Toklas called letter writing
her "work," and she did it extremely well. She
had a kind of genius for it. The epistolary art is
the art of favorable self-representation; Toklas
emerges from her letters as a great lady, witty,
self-deprecating, attentive, cultivated. Her for-
ays into what Henry James called "the twaddle
of graciousness" are especially masterful. Here
she is thanking W. G. Rogers for a gift parcel
she received from him and his wife, Mildred, in
March 1947:

I went into the bed room and there was the
package—I was so excited I forgot my exhaustion and boredom and opened it feverishly
(but carefully undoing the string). And there
were all the treasures—no I just couldn't believe my eyes—the wonderful towels—the
warm combies (not a darn—*new new new*) the
lavender soap (sweet but naughty Mildred
Kiddie) and then oh then the utterly lovely
scarf. I never thought to see anything like it
again—to say nothing of having it for my own.
It's a royal gift and it's overwhelmingly beautiful. In the evening I had a visit from my
young Turkish painter and I gave him a long
lecture on the simplicity and at the same time
subtlety of the American gift—the unerring
taste—the appreciation of métier and quality
that no European realizes or will accept.

In another letter of thanks—this one for
an "exquisite nosegay holder"—the twaddle
becomes intertwined with a piece of history,
and a grudge. "Never have I seen anything so
lovely and it gives me so much pleasure," Toklas writes to her friend Louise Taylor in January 1947, and goes on,

You see when the Germans came . . . and then—well we won't go into that—they took a great many things but not a picture—not a drawing—not a piece of furniture—so that Gertrude wouldn't ever let me mention anything about it ever because she said we had got off mighty easily—and of course she was right. She absolutely used the pictures every minute of the day and so that was alright— but the rooms lacked the prettiness and elegance they had and sometimes I minded it secretly. . . . And now my dear—all the missing elegance has returned and I thank you very deeply.

What Toklas "won't go into" and what Gertrude "wouldn't ever let me mention" is the looting of decorative objects, silver, linens, and utensils from the apartment on rue Christine during the pair's wartime absence. The painting collection remained in place. There was a moment of danger in July 1944, when four Gestapo men broke into the apartment and threatened to cut up and burn the Picassos, which they saw as *saloperie juive*. A resourceful neighbor called the French police, who were able to dispatch the Gestapo men by asking them for requisition orders that they did not have. (When the police arrived, the Gestapo men were in Stein's bedroom trying on her Chinese coats.) A longer-term reprieve for the paintings was achieved by Stein and Toklas's protector, Bernard Faÿ, who now used his influence to protect the art. But no one protected the pretty things that Toklas cherished. (In her memoir, she notes that a little petit-point footstool she had made after a design by Picasso and a pair of Louis XV silver candlesticks were among the objects stolen from the apartment.) In her tour de force of resentment against Stein, swathed in yards of silky compliment to Louise Taylor, Toklas permits us a poignant glimpse of her position as the wife of a willful genius.

However, one of the most astute of Toklas's young men, the classics professor and critic Donald Sutherland, questions whether Toklas ever actually played the wife-of-a-genius role as it is supposed to be played. In his memoir *Alice and Gertrude and Others* (1971), Sutherland tells this story:

The self-effacement which Alice was supposed
to have cultivated and which indeed was carried so far that her very existence was de-
bated in the press, became a form of publicity
in itself, and if she did subordinate herself to
Gertrude, in public at least, she was not at all
the sort willingly to disappear. I had been put
straight about her existence long ago, when I
turned up at the apartment with a large bouquet of small roses for Gertrude. I did something that should have been unpardonable: I
gave the bouquet to Alice at the door as one
would give it to a maid who would then fetch
a vase for it. But Alice brought the bouquet
and me at once into the living room, saying,
"Look, Lovey, what Donald has brought me!
Thank you so much. How did you know these
are just my favorite flowers?" Then she went
to get a vase.

Sutherland was put straight about Tok-
las's steel, but, like Joan Chapman, and every-
one else who knew both women, he preferred
Stein's gold. During a final visit he makes to
Toklas in 1966, an extraordinary memory of
Stein comes to him. Toklas has brought up

Hemingway and says, "You know, I made Gertrude get rid of him."

> "I know," I said. I knew it, not only by inference from the book [*A Moveable Feast*], I also knew something we had never discussed, that the relation between Gertrude Stein and Hemingway was more than literary comradeship at one time or even than maternal and filial affection. I had heard that Hemingway had not infrequently said in conversation and once at least in a letter that he had always wanted to lay her.

The letter Sutherland means was written to W. G. Rogers on the occasion of the publication of *When This You See Remember Me*. Hemingway wrote: "She used to talk to me about homosexuality and how it was fine in and for women and no good in men and I used to listen and learn and I always wanted to fuck her and she knew it."

Sutherland goes on, "I could well believe it, for the second time I met her she came too close and my sexual response was both unequivocal and, considering that I was nineteen and she sixty, bewildering. She said in a book I was very nervous when we first met; nervous would be no word for me the second time."

Has the book dropped from the reader's hand? Has anything prepared him for Sutherland's erection? Hemingway's line is the sort of macho showing off one expects of him and only half believes. But Sutherland's account has the ring of whole truth. Fattuski (as Stein called herself in "Lifting Belly") was obviously a powerfully sexy woman, attractive to men as well as to women. It was no wonder that Alice was jealous of everyone, male or female, who "came too close."[6]

Sutherland and Toklas are having their conversation about Hemingway at her apartment, but it is not the elegant flat to which Doda Conrad came for tea and from which Roubina snatched the great paintings. Toklas has been evicted from 5 rue Christine and is living in an austere fifth-floor flat in a modern building on rue de la Convention that Doda Conrad and Janet Flanner found for her. She is old and disabled. The threat of eviction had been hanging over her for many years, but she

disregarded it, thinking she could beat it.
When 5 rue Christine was sold, she turned
down the chance to buy her apartment, believing herself safe as an elderly statutory tenant.
However, French law dictated that an apartment could not remain vacant for more than
four months, and when Toklas was in Rome for
the winter of 1960–61 the apartment's owners
made their move to expel her, filing eviction
papers. She fought the expulsion for several
years in the only way she knew—by getting
influential people to intervene. In May 1963,
Toklas wrote to Sutherland, "Jo Barry and
Doda Conrad are at work. Doda is getting Malraux to work. It appears he's all powerful! Made-
leine thinks that if General de Gaulle is not going
to save me I had better go to a hotel at once."
But once again, even Malraux and de Gaulle
couldn't make the impossible possible. Toklas
was able to fend off the eviction for another
year, but in November of 1964 it took place.

Sutherland was part of the group led by the
forceful Doda Conrad that looked after the
destitute, aged Toklas. In *Alice and Gertrude
and Others,* he writes of visiting Toklas in 1965

at a nursing home where she is recovering from a broken hip. He finds her "sitting up in an armchair, dressed in a dressing gown which was not fresh and on which she had dribbled." He asks her "as delicately as I could" about her finances and learns that "she was penniless, without even the pin-money to send a maid out for a newspaper or a bottle of toilet water." Sutherland thrusts a few hundred francs into her purse and then reflects on the general problem of looking after Alice. The friends who have established a fund are afraid of putting it into her hands, lest she "spend it foolishly and run through it in a few months or less." Conrad writes in his memoir, "It was difficult to satisfy Alice Toklas's tastes, which were still extravagant. I remember tricking her by having fruit bought at the market and having it brought to her in used bags from Fauchon or Hédiard. This gave her the illusion of eating the best food Paris had to offer and of giving her visitors sherry of noble origins." But Sutherland's own fears are not about fancy food— they are about Catholic dogma. He worries about Toklas's worry that her plan of meeting

Gertrude in Heaven will go awry unless palms are greased. According to Catholic dogma, the unbaptized Stein is in Limbo. "How did one go about getting Gertrude out of Limbo? . . . With enough prayer, enough masses and candles, enough penitence, Gertrude could be sprung and settled in Purgatory to await Alice before they went on together to Heaven. It could be made very expensive, and it is possible that if Alice had a perfectly free hand, all or most of the Picasso collection would now be in the Vatican Museum." Sutherland ends his mordant aria by noting of Toklas that "her own salvation was endangered now, for her confessor, finding her without money, had ceased to visit her."

Virgil Thomson, in his 1966 autobiography, records a conversation with Gertrude Stein about a difference he saw between Jews and Christians. Jews, Thomson said, are always breaking up with their friends while Christians make up after quarrels. "The explanation I offered for such independent behavior was that the Jewish religion, though it sets aside a day for private Atonement, offers no mechanics for forgiveness. . . . When a Christian, on the other hand, knows he has done wrong to anyone, he is obliged in all honesty to attempt restitution; and the person he has wronged must thereupon forgive." Stein took no umbrage at the slyly anti-Semitic comparison. In fact, she "liked this explanation, and for nearly twenty years it remained our convention." Thomson adds,

> It was not until after Gertrude's death that Alice said one day, "You and Gertrude had it settled between you as to why Jews don't make up their quarrels, and I went along with you. But now I've found a better reason for it. Gertrude was right, of course, to believe that 'when a Jew dies he's dead.' And that's exactly why Jews don't need to make up. When we've had enough of someone we can get rid of him. You Christians can't, because you've got to spend eternity together."

We can get rid of him. The "we" leaps off the page. In no other memoir, in no letter or

book or article does Toklas identify herself as a
Jew. (After her conversion, she was quick to assume a Christian identity; the term "our Lord
Jesus" rolled easily off her pen in a letter written the day after her admission to the Church.)
It seems likely that in her remarks to Thomson
Toklas maintained her customary distance
from her tribe, and that Thomson—not realizing that Toklas was a Jew with explanations—
interpolated the "we." Toklas was hardly the
only Jew to pretend she wasn't one. She was
born into an anti-Semitic world—one that not
only produced Hitler but tolerated low-grade
anti-Semitism among even its most civilized
members. Here, for example, is the civilized
Donald Sutherland, writing to Thornton Wilder's sister, Isabel, about Toklas's biographer:
"I want to ask you about one Linda Simon. . . .
Is she the impossibly preemptive Jewess she
sounds like, or something else?" Linda Simon
is a reserved, soft-spoken professor of English
literature at Skidmore College who is as far as
it is possible to be from the pushy yenta of
Sutherland's imaginings. When she told me of
the rebuffs she received while working on her

book on Toklas thirty years ago, she attributed them to her youth and inexperience, but after reading Sutherland's letter, I wondered whether being Jewish was held against her as well.

In *When This You See Remember Me* Rogers writes of a car trip in the French countryside with Stein and Toklas—during which the two women constantly fought. Every arrangement was an occasion for dispute. Stein was the naughty child who wants to have fun no matter what, and Toklas was the grownup with tightly compressed lips. "While few people question Miss Stein's genius, not so much has been heard about Miss Toklas's. If one is the creative spirit, the other is the immensely practical spirit," Rogers tactfully writes, and goes on: "It was as if Miss Stein's practical sense had been removed from her person and deposited in the person of Miss Toklas. The ego was in the front seat"—Stein did the driving: dangerously—"and the alter ego in the back.

The battle which most geniuses fight within themselves was exteriorized and fought openly between her and her friend." "Do you not get tired of always being right?" Stein wrote in an abstruse late work called *The Geographical History of America*—surely, on some level, addressing Toklas.

Posterity has not dealt kindly with Stein's alter ego. Deep mythic structures determine who is likable and who isn't among the famous dead. The practical spirit is an essential but unlovable spirit. Toklas remains the dour ugly crone to Stein's handsome playful princess. The memoirists who profess to love Toklas (only Doda Conrad leveled about his feelings) allow their distaste to leak out. Sutherland cannot spare her the robe on which she had dribbled. Donald Windham notices that as she chews artichokes in a restaurant she is "unaware that the oil is running down her chin." Doda Conrad, also watching Toklas eat, likens her to "a little voracious, ravenous animal throwing itself on its food, eyes fixed on the other half of the bite she had just swallowed for fear that it might escape!" Toklas's efforts to secure Life Everlasting may have succeeded, but her hopes of being kindly remembered on earth have fallen short. As Gertrude Stein said, Life is funny that way.

NOTES

1. A preliminary notebook at the Beinecke Library shows Stein struggling to master the Toklas voice, and going hopelessly astray:

"I myself have had no liking for violence but in spite of that which is what I wish to say I have had some occasions to feel what violence is and when I do feel so I can and have thoroughly tempted there which is what there is to do.

"Moreover nobody can doubt if it is not to be considered to have which is the result I have had that I have what I have and I always have as I always will had to have that which I have. In this way there can be no doubt, no doubt, that in no way there is any doubt that having to have that which I have I have had and I have that which I have."

In the next notebook Stein finds her way to the celebrated passage: "I myself have had no liking for violence and have always enjoyed the pleasures of needlework and gardening. I am fond of paintings, furniture, tapestry, houses and flowers even vegetables and fruit-trees. I like a view but I like to sit with my back turned to it."

The preliminary notebook was discovered and transcribed by Ulla Dydo.

2. Hilary Corke, "Reflections on a Great Stone Face," *Kenyon Review* 23 (Summer 1961).

3. Daniel Henry Kahnweiler was the German Jewish art dealer who began to represent the Cubists in his gallery in Paris before their work was valuable; he had difficulties in World War I because of his Germanness and in World War II because of his Jewishness.

4. In their appendix essay, Burns and Dydo note that "from July 1940 until June 1944, Faÿ was an editor of the only journal financed by the Germans, the anti-Jewish *La Gerbe.*"

5. Stein returned to Claribel Cone's "passion for comfort" thirty years later in *The Autobiography of Alice B. Toklas,* where she told this story about her: "She liked ease and graciousness and comfort. She and her sister Etta Cone were traveling. The only room in the hotel was not comfortable. Etta bade her sister put up with it as it was only for one night. Etta, answered Doctor Claribel, one night is as important as any other night in my life and I must be comfortable." In 1923, in a piece called "Subject-Cases: The Background of a Detective Story," Stein wrote: "Fortune and as comfortably, this night is as important as any other night and as

comfortable fortunately. Fortunately as fortunately, as fortunate it was fortunate it was very fortunate, fortunately. This night was as important as any other night fortunately."

6. Ulla Dydo, in the course of trying to decipher a hermetic piece called "An Elucidation," through the study of Stein's notebooks, came to a surprising conclusion about Stein and Toklas's sex life. She found reason to think that Stein regularly gave Toklas orgasms—called "cows" in the notebooks—but received none herself. "Her own sexual feelings," Dydo writes in *The Language That Rises*, "always have a babyish and cuddly tone. Baby does not experience orgasms but wants cuddling." This is a remarkable reversal of roles: outside the bedroom Toklas does all the work—she is cook, housekeeper, typist, secretary—but in bed it is Stein who labors; she calls herself "the best cow giver in all the world."

ILLUSTRATION
CREDITS

The publisher gratefully acknowledges permission to reproduce photographs from the following: Carl Mydans/Getty Images, page 184; Carl Van Vechten, courtesy of the Carl Van Vechten Trust, pages 154 and 194; Cecil Beaton, courtesy of the Cecil Beaton Studio Archive at Sotheby's, page ii, the Estate of Gertrude Stein, through its Literary Executor, Stanford Gann, Jr., of Levin & Gann, P.A., endpapers and pages 22, 33, 37, 44, 76, and 117; Man Ray, © Man Ray Trust/Artists Rights Society (ARS), NY/ADAGP, Paris, pages 15 and 46; and Yale Collection of American Literature, New Haven, Beinecke Rare Book and Manuscript Library, endpapers and pages 15, 22, 33, 37, 46, 76, and 117.

Alice Toklas

Only person in her or Alice in
my experience is Zobel, she is
low clean through to the bottom
crooked, a liar of the most
sordid millennic undramatic
unimaginative prostitute
type, coward, ungenerous, con-
conscienceless, mean, vulgarly
triumphant and remorseless,
caddish, in short just